D0976310

One-Moment Meditation

ALSO BY MARTIN BOROSON

Becoming Me: a story of creation

One-Moment Meditation

Stillness for People on the Go

Martin Boroson

Winter Road Publishing

NEW YORK

Copyright © 2007, 2009 Martin Boroson
All rights reserved.
ISBN 978-0-9823746-0-3
Library of Congress Control Number: 2009923064

Published in the United States
by Winter Road Publishing
Port Jefferson Station, NY

For distribution information contact:
sales@winterroadpublishing.com
or Baker & Taylor at 1-800-775-1800

All rights reserved. No part of this publication may be reproduced,
stored in a retrieval system, or transmitted in any form or by any means,
electronic, mechanical, photocopying, recording or otherwise, without
the prior permission of the copyright owner.

FIRST EDITION
Design by Level C

First published in 2007 in the United Kingdom by Rider, an imprint of
Ebury Publishing, Random House, under the title *The One-Moment
Master: Stillness for People on the Go.*

for my parents,
Florence and Louis Boroson,
with love

With a man's dying breath,
he should be prepared to make a fresh start.

Nikos Kazantzakis (attrib.)

Contents

Part 3: The Moment in Time

Part 4: Advanced Training

Part 5: Meeting the Moment

Part 6: Very Advanced Training

Part 7: The Miracle of the Moment

Part 8: Mastering the Moment

Introduction

Think of all the moments we "lose"—stuck in traffic, standing in line, sitting in a boring meeting. Think of all the moments we "waste"—going to parties we don't enjoy, working when we're not focused, watching one more television show before bed. Then there are those "stolen moments"—the moments we grab when no one's looking—to window shop, surf the net, or fiddle with our phones. And then there are those moments that pass by unnoticed—the moments between other moments. What if each of these moments offered us an opportunity? What if each and every moment offered us a chance to become more calm, alert, balanced and content? What if there were something simple we could do, in just a moment, that could have a profound effect on our lives?

•   •   •

This book was conceived in a moment.

I was meditating one morning for my usual thirty minutes, and was determined to sit still, eyes looking down, for the full thirty minutes. But this particular morning, I was restless, my mind was racing, and time seemed to be moving so slowly. I worried that I had forgotten to set the alarm, and that I might end up sitting there for hours. It certainly felt like hours. I wanted to check the clock. Many times. But I was determined to sit still, and just didn't want to give in. Then I gave in.

I turned to the clock and discovered that I had not forgotten to set the alarm. There was one minute left. Which meant that I'd just spent twenty-nine minutes wondering if thirty minutes had passed. Discouraged, I thought, "With just a minute left, I might as well quit for today." And then it hit me: "What's wrong with a minute of meditation? What did I hope to experience in thirty minutes that I can't experience in one minute?" So I decided to start again, as if from the beginning. I decided to meditate for whatever time was left. I decided to meditate for a minute . . . but make it a good one.

From that moment on, my attitude toward time began to change. I began to think less about long-term goals and more about present opportunities. I began to realize how much could be achieved in a very short time. And I began to meditate in a new way—not just sitting on my cushion each morning for thirty minutes, but briefly, all throughout my day, wherever I happened to be—on the train, at my desk, at the gym. I began to understand that the more quickly I could tap into peacefulness, and the fewer props I needed, the better. In short, I began to meditate whenever I had a moment.

• • •

Most of the time, we fail to realize the enormous potential of a moment. Perhaps this is because we think of a moment as a very short amount of time—just a few seconds—and therefore rather negligible. But the word "moment" actually comes from a Latin word that means "a particle sufficient to turn the scales." In other words, a moment can be revolutionary. It can turn your life around. A moment is, by its very nature, momentous.

Imagine what can happen in a moment: a dam bursts, the earth quakes, a dry forest bursts into flames. In just a moment, a drunk driver speeds through a stop sign and hits your car. In just a moment, stock prices start tumbling. You never know when something that you take for granted will be gone.

But a moment can also bring healing, inspiration, and joy. In just a moment, a fantastic new idea lands, unexpectedly, in your mind. In just a moment, someone solves a problem for you, or you get a phone call from a long-lost friend. In just a moment, after years of division, a wall comes down. In just a moment, during a long illness, you simply start recovering, and no one can say exactly why.

But whether life-changing moments are happy or sad, global or personal, they remind us that ordinary life has the possibility to be extraordinary. In just a moment, ordinary life can crack open to reveal another reality that was inconceivable the moment before. In other words, dramatic change doesn't require a lot of time: it only takes a moment.

I have helped many individuals and organizations through processes of major change. And although these processes can take time, when the breakthroughs do happen, they happen suddenly, in a moment. No one can predict when they will happen or what they will be. But the best condition for having a breakthrough is when the people involved are truly present in the present moment, and open to its possibility. In other words, they are open to the radical possibility that no matter what their plans, habits, or expectations might be, *this* moment offers the potential for significant change.

●   ●   ●

This book will help you notice the moment, understand the moment, appreciate the moment, be in the moment, and tap the enormous potential of a moment. And it won't take a lot of time. The first exercise requires no more than one or two minutes each day—guaranteed. As you progress, this exercise actually gets shorter and shorter, taking less and less time, until you can do it in just a moment.

With this approach, you will be able to refresh and recharge yourself many times throughout the day. You will learn to experience deep stillness (which is your nature) in the midst of activity (which is also your nature). You will understand time in a new way, and learn ways to transform a day that feels crowded and rushed into one that feels spacious and full of opportunity.

As you practice these techniques, and your understanding of this philosophy deepens, you will approach what could be called mastery of the moment. Mastery, in this case, does not mean dominating the moment or taking control of it. Nor does it mean submitting to the moment or letting it control you. It simply means being at peace in the moment—that there is no tension between you and whatever is happening right now.

I have taught this technique in lectures and workshops, on the radio, in leadership seminars, and in on-the-job training sessions, and have seen how it can benefit people in many different ways. If you are new to meditation, this technique gives you a straightforward method that will fit in easily with your life as it is. If you have tried meditation and "failed," this technique gives you a way to try again—a way that focuses not on long-term success but on short-term opportunity. And if you believe that you are just "too busy to meditate," this approach takes away that excuse: everyone has a moment to spare.

Although this book was written with beginners in mind, it was also written for advanced beginners. (Advanced beginners are people so advanced that they are always willing to begin again.) So even if you are experienced at mediation, I hope that you will be open to this approach. You might well find that it helps you to refresh and reinvigorate your existing practice, or to integrate that practice into the challenges of everyday life. And if you are one of those experienced meditators who get hung up on "how long you can sit still without thinking" (a kind of meditation machismo), this approach will remind you to take everything—even meditation—one moment at a time.

●　　●　　●

Is it really possible to meditate in a moment?

Many people do see mediation as an endurance test: the longer they can sit still, being peaceful, the more spiritual they are. Many people also believe that meditation must be practiced in a serene and beautiful retreat—far removed from everyday life. They have these beliefs, no doubt, because so much of our spiritual heritage has been handed down by monks, nuns, hermits, and prophets—people who renounced ordinary life to spend years and years in silent contemplation.

But times are changing, and our understanding of meditation is, too. Scientific research is confirming that the benefits of meditation are not just esoteric or "spiritual," but quite practical, too. Laboratory experiments and psychological studies have shown that meditation can improve our mood, decrease anxiety, alleviate depression, lower blood pressure, strengthen the immune system, and promote optimism and resilience.

Today, more and more people believe that the benefits of meditation should be available to us when we need them, and that the practice of meditation should be do-able everywhere— whether we're stuck in traffic, starting a business, or changing a diaper. Many people today also want to bring meditation, or meditative principles, into their relationships, their parenting, and their work, and see a need for more meditative approaches in politics, business decisions, and public conversations. Surely the more quickly we can be peaceful, and the fewer props we need, the better. So let me tell you why I believe that it is not only possible to meditate in a moment, but essential that we do.

We all fantasize, from time to time, about being peaceful in some *other* time or place. We imagine being peaceful in the future—at the end of the day, on the weekend, after the kids grow up, when we retire. Or we imagine being peaceful somewhere else—in church, in a park, on that deserted beach. But each time we do this, we fail to meet the moment that is here. We let ourselves off the hook. This is an especially self-defeating form of procrastination, for the moment in which we most need to be peaceful is the very moment in which it is not so easy to be peaceful.

Also, whenever we think that peacefulness takes a lot of time, or will come only in the future, we are focusing on *becoming* peaceful rather than *being* peaceful. We are keeping ourselves in a state of "wanting," and this state of wanting is, by definition, not a state of being or "having." So if you believe that you must meditate for a long time in order to become peaceful, you are creating more stress for yourself. It's like throwing a ball out in front of you, then racing to catch it, and then if you do catch it, immediately throwing it out in front of you again—while also complaining that you never ever have a ball.

On a deeper level, if our sense of contentment is dependent on circumstances, then it is vulnerable to a change of circumstances. If we are only content because life is going well, we will not be content when life is going badly. That's just not a very stable or deep kind of contentment. True contentment transcends the "ups and downs" of life. It embraces life as it is now, with all of its imperfections. In other words, the only way to be really peaceful is to be fully content with what's happening now—even if, sometimes, it isn't peaceful.

In the wonderfully succinct words of the spiritual teacher Krishnamurti, "It's now or never." This doesn't mean that if you aren't feeling peaceful now, you will never feel peaceful. It just means that contentment is only possible when you are not throwing that ball into the future. It is only possible in the present tense (or rather, the present *not-tensed*). When you are truly present in the present, your mind is not concerned with wanting things to be different than they are—and *that* is contentment.

Since contentment can only be found now, in the present moment, this also means that *it doesn't take any time at all*. It doesn't happen over time: it happens in a moment. So you don't have to go on a retreat or quit your job or find "twenty minutes, twice a day" in order to become peaceful. Peace is *always* available. It is offering itself to you now, now, and now again, wherever you are. But you aren't aware of it because, well, you're too busy doing other things, like trying to become peaceful (or reading this book).

So think of my approach as just going straight to the point. If being peaceful is possible now, and is only possible now, then you might as well get right to it. But please know that I don't intend this approach to replace any other form of meditation or prayer, any path of self-discovery, or any of the excellent self-help or leadership books available today. It's just that whatever path you choose, whatever help you seek, if you don't learn to master the moment, then your chance of success is limited. But if you *do* learn to master the moment, well, then there's nothing stopping you.

• • •

At the heart of this book is the moment. But because a moment is quite elusive, and can seem to go by so quickly, you might have trouble finding it. That's why, in Part 1, *Basic Training*, you will begin with something easier to get your head around:

a minute. (A minute is like a moment with handles on either side. You know where it begins and ends, so it's easier to grasp.) With the first exercise in this book, The Basic Minute, you will learn how to experience stillness in just a minute.

Part 2, *Intermediate Training*, then shows you how to make The Basic Minute more versatile. It becomes a tool that you can use wherever you are, no matter what is happening, even in an emergency. Part 3, *The Moment in Time*, is more philosophical. It explores our perceptions of time and the nature of time, showing you just how flexible time can be. Part 4, *Advanced Training*, then teaches you how to reduce the length of a Basic Minute step by step, until you can experience its benefits in almost a moment. Part 5, *Meeting the Moment*, explores the deeper meaning of a moment, and gives you examples of some extraordinary ones. In Part 6, *Very Advanced Training*, you will learn how to experience stillness all around you, all the time, in everything you do. Part 7, *The Miracle of the Moment*, gives you several flexible and playful techniques that will help you tap the miraculous potential of each moment. And finally, in Part 8, *Mastering the Moment*, you will be challenged to take one last little leap into mastery.

Although the chapters in this book are short, they are highly concentrated—so please don't gulp them down. (If you do, you might get spiritual indigestion, a common condition caused by reading too many big ideas without assimilating them.) The best way to read this book is slowly. Read a chapter, chew it over, then read it again. Practice the exercises. Live with them.

When you've digested them fully and are hungry for more, go on to the next chapter.

You may, however, prefer to read the book all the way through first, to get an overview. That's fine, too. But let me just caution you that if you do rush ahead to the end, you might not understand it fully. That's because the way I describe and define a moment deepens as the book progresses. Each chapter is written with the assumption that you've changed a bit since practicing the exercises in the previous chapter. In other words, the end of this book is written for a different *you*.

Do make a serious commitment to practicing these exercises seriously, but please don't take too them seriously. Approach them as play rather than penance, and feel free to adapt them to suit your life. There's just no telling what will work for you. Or when.

There is so much about the moment, and the nature of time, that is mysterious and paradoxical and impossible to explain or even understand. Not everything in this book will make sense to you all the time; sometimes it doesn't make sense to me. So you may want to put this book away for a while and then come back to it, sometime later, for another dip. You might see it completely differently.

In the spirit of simplicity, I have avoided using citations and studies and religious language and diagrams and flowcharts and tables and cross-cultural comparisons. Just try the exercises for yourself. You won't need to quit your job, get a babysitter, or even find a cabin by the pond. You won't need to buy any special clothing. You won't need to keep a journal. You won't need to join a group, get any unusual equipment, reorganize your office, download a program, or buy an instructional DVD from my website. All you need is here—right where you are.

PART 1
Basic Training

In this first part of the book, you will learn the Basic Minute, the foundation of the One-Moment Method. The first chapter introduces you to this exercise and the following chapters help to deepen your experience and understanding of it.

You might think there is a lot of detail here for what is, after all, just a minute. But the Basic Minute, because it is so condensed, requires the same level of skill that you might otherwise need for an exercise that takes an hour.

The more you practice the Minute, the more subtlety you will discover there. For example, there are some aspects of the Minute, such as breathing and posture, which seem fairly obvious at first but become more intriguing over time. Or you might find that your Minute feels crowded when you are first learning it, but seems more spacious over time, as your mind slows down—even though it still only takes a minute.

The Basic Minute

For the Basic Minute, you will need to have a timer or alarm that can be set for one minute exactly. (A kitchen timer is ideal.) Later in this training, you will dispense with the timer, but for now, it's essential.

You will also need to find a time and place in which you won't be disturbed by anyone else. Treat the Minute as if something truly profound will be experienced there, even though it's just a minute. Be open to the possibility—in the words of Sufi poet, Jalal al-din Rumi—that:

A little while alone in your room
will prove more valuable
than anything else that could ever be given to you.[1]

In practical terms, this means: shut the door and turn off your phone. Close down your email and lower the volume on your answering machine. Put a sign on the door: *Back in a Minute*. In other words, press the "pause button" on your life. For just a minute. Realize that there are few things so urgent that they can't wait a minute.

Now that you have carved out a minute of solitude, sit down. It's best to choose a hard surface, like the edge of a chair or a firm cushion on the floor, so you don't slouch or slump. And make sure you're not leaning on anything, like the arms of a chair: it's up to you now.

Now for your legs. Choose any position that feels balanced, symmetrical and stable, a position that you can hold without shifting for a minute. If you're sitting on the floor, try crossing both of your legs. If you're sitting on a chair, just plant your feet firmly on the floor or hook them around the chair legs. (Try not to leave one foot dangling in the air, or it might start bouncing without your consent.) But whichever position you choose, the key principle is this: when you sit in a way that is balanced, stable and still, you are practicing *being* balanced, stable and still.

Now that you are sitting down, sit up. Imagine that the crown of your head is being pulled upward, away from the ground. Don't do this forcefully; just gently encourage your spine to lengthen. This may feel like a stretch, but think of it this way: for as long as you've been on earth, gravity has been pulling you down, so it takes some determination to lift yourself up. Gradually, this will become second nature. You will shed the weight of the world. Think of it as cosmic traction.

Now that you are sitting up, relax. The more familiar you are with this position, the more quickly this will happen: your head moves up and everything else eases out. Your organs settle into place. Your lungs have a bit more room to do their job.

Now set your alarm for one minute exactly. You may think it's silly to use an alarm for just one minute, but it really is necessary. The alarm helps you to forget about time, while also ensuring that you don't drift off. Don't even think that you can do the Basic Minute while keeping one eye on the clock. It's essential that, for just a minute, you yield control of time completely—and this requires an alarm.

You might be tempted to set your alarm for more than a minute, on the theory that you'll get more from the exercise if you do it longer. Please don't. This exercise is intended to convince you that you can indeed experience genuine peacefulness in just a minute. So if you sit there longer, you're missing the point.

Now for your hands. For most of the day, your hands are very busy doing and expressing, often without your knowledge. But in the Basic Minute, you want to harness all your energy into one place. So try placing one hand on each knee, or placing both hands in your lap, one on top of the other. There are many different ways to do this, but the most important thing is that your hands be balanced, symmetrical and still, just like your legs.

Now close your eyes. Breathe in and out gently through your nose. If that feels odd, or you have a cold, it's okay to breathe through your mouth. It doesn't matter whether your inhalation is longer than your exhalation, or vice versa. The only thing that matters is that you take one breath in and one breath out, one after the other, over and over again.

Now bring all your attention to your breathing. For some people, the idea of "paying attention" triggers an alarm response, as if there were an inner drill sergeant yelling, "Sit up and pay attention." This is not the best attitude for the Basic Minute, because it immediately triggers conflict and fear, and these are not conducive to peacefulness. So a better instruction might be "focus on your breathing."

But there's a problem with this, too. To "focus on your breathing" suggests work, and that brings up the possibility of failure, another dynamic that's not too helpful here. It also suggests a split between your mind and your breathing—that your mind is *here* and your breathing is *there*. With an assumption like that, you will never experience "all of you" being in the same place at the same time.

So it might be better to say "drop your mind into your breathing" or "rest your mind in your breathing" or "immerse yourself in your breathing" or my favorite: "allow your mind to settle into your breathing." Use whichever instruction suits you best.

Now let me say a word about breathing. For as long as you *are*, you are breathing. Your body may roam and your mind may wander, but your breathing is always present, right where you are. In the Basic Minute, you are simply choosing to settle your mind into something that is always present.

In Latin, the word for breath is *spiritus*, which is where we get the words *spirit, inspire* and *inspiration*. This suggests that there is something quite spiritual about breathing, and indeed many practices, such as yoga, explore this aspect of breathing in great depth. But in the Basic Minute, it's best not to think about anything spiritual. Just think about nothing. Just be present in your breathing with full attention. Do this, and this alone, until the alarm sounds.

Because this exercise only takes one minute, please make the most of it. Even with your total commitment, however, it's quite likely that, even in the space of one minute, you will lose focus. You will forget about your breathing. You'll start thinking about all sorts of things. You may wonder: am I really so scatter-brained? Yes. We all are. Don't worry about it. When you realize you have become distracted, don't condemn yourself or think any more about it. Just think, "Hmm," and settle your mind back in your breathing. This may happen many times in the space of a minute, but just keep coming back to your breathing until the alarm sounds. Then stop. You're done.

It's perfectly fine to do the Basic Minute several times a day, but the important thing is to make a commitment to do at least one Basic Minute—as an anchor—every day. But please don't set yourself up for failure, either. With so many resolutions, when we can't stick to them we feel that we have failed, and then our sense of failure eats away at us until, well, we try again, with just a little bit less enthusiasm next time.

The Basic Minute is entirely unlike that. First of all, it only takes a minute, so you probably *can* do it every day. Second, if you miss a day or two, there's no problem, because the Minute isn't really cumulative. It's not like counting calories or running a race or trying to achieve a sales target. And it's not like quitting smoking, where one lapse can set you back a year. With the Basic Minute, there is no requirement that if you miss a day you have to go back to the beginning. The reason for this is that every time you do the Basic Minute, you should make a fresh start, as if it were the first time. (The more you do it, the better you become at starting all over again.)

So even if you're able to do the Minute every day, try to think of each time as the first time. Consider each Minute a fresh start and approach each Minute with an open mind. If you have a minute today, just try it. If you have a minute tomorrow, just try it. And if you have a minute the next day, just try it. In fact, why not try it right now?

The Basic Minute

1. Create a place of solitude.

2. Sit down.

3. Place your legs in a relaxed but fixed position.

4. Sit up.

5. Set your alarm for exactly one minute.

6. Place your hands in a relaxed but fixed position.

7. Close your eyes.

8. Allow your mind to settle into your breathing.

9. When the alarm sounds, stop.

Understanding
the Minute

One of the things I loved most about smoking cigarettes, when I smoked cigarettes, was that it gave me so many times each day for a little pause. At my peak, I managed to pack in about twenty pauses a day. Smoking provided such a good cover for doing nothing. Even if I smoked while doing something else, there was at least one moment of stillness when I withdrew my attention from what I was doing in order to light the cigarette and inhale deeply. In a bizarre way, this was a contemplative experience. Nowadays, those of us who have quit smoking just barrel through the day without any break at all, just like everyone else. The Basic Minute is a little bit like a cigarette break—without the cigarette.

The Basic Minute is a structure that enables you to have a deep experience of *just being*. The Basic Minute is not a time for being this or being that. It's not a time for making decisions or worrying about life. It's not a time for being complicated. For one structured minute, instead of all that *doing*—the normal frenzy of activity—you are quite deliberately *just being*. It is like a state of suspension: for one whole minute, everything is on hold. You step out of time and come back to your life refreshed.

The Basic Minute, however, is not just about stopping *doing*: it's also about stopping *youing*. Don't get me wrong: there's nothing wrong with being you, but it sure can take a lot of effort, and from time to time, you deserve a break from yourself.

Now the first time you do a Minute, you may not find it so remarkable. But think of it as a dipstick that you use each day to tap a deep well of peace. The more you relax into the Minute, and trust it, the more peace you will discover there. There may be days when you only get a drop. But you are still tapping an unlimited resource.

As you practice the Minute, you may discover some curious things about time. The Minute might seem frustratingly long if you are worried about something or if you're eager to get back to work. Or the Minute might go by too quickly and leave you wanting more. You might be amazed at how busy your mind can be sometimes. Or you might be amazed at how big a break you can get from your mind in just one Minute. Eventually, you may experience a kind of infinity even within the otherwise strict boundaries of a Minute: for one minute of clock time, time stretched.

The Basic Minute is quite different from some of the other self-help methods around today, so let me add some clarifications. The Basic Minute is not about *the power of positive thinking*. Nor is it about *orienting* your life or *affirming* something that you are or would like to be. Nor is it about *success*.

Nor is it about *intention*—other than the intention to have a little break from intending. True, if you practice the Minute regularly, you might find yourself thinking more positively and liking yourself more. You might find that you are indeed getting what you want—or at least liking what you have. You might start feeling more successful and that your intentions are clearer and more in harmony with the world. But just remember that the Basic Minute isn't *about* anything and it isn't *for* anything. In fact, the Basic Minute *isn't* anything at all. It's just nothing. Just one whole minute of nothing. That's why it's such a relief.

Before going on, please do a Basic Minute.

Where and When

In time, you will learn to achieve the benefits of a Basic Minute on the go—in many different places and at many different times. But for now, it's helpful to have a particular time and place—let's call it a *timeplace*—in which to practice the Basic Minute every day. (If you travel frequently, and are rarely in the same time and place, it's okay to improvise.)

Many people like to dedicate an area in their home for meditation or prayer, or visit somewhere outside their home that they consider sacred. But none of this is necessary for the Basic Minute: there are many quite ordinary timeplaces that work well. In this chapter, I will suggest some timeplaces that you might try and will discuss some of their differences.

After waking/before sleeping

Doing the Basic Minute just after waking up is a great way to start the day truly fresh, before the stresses and strains of the day get a hold on you. Doing the Basic Minute before going to sleep is a way to clear your mind and end the day fresh . . . after the stresses and strains of the day have got hold of you.

In nature

Most people find that being in nature helps them calm down. So by all means, if you have access to a park, backyard, garden, farm, forest, or even just a tree, try to do the Basic Minute there. But don't get too fixed on doing the Minute in nature. You can do the Basic Minute anywhere that you can find some solitude.

My friend, Elise Thoron, a New Yorker, was once walking in the direction of St. Stephen's Green, a park in the center of Ireland's capital city, Dublin. It was 12:50 in the afternoon, ten minutes before everyone routinely took their lunch break. An older gentleman rushed passed her in a terrible hurry. This was back in 1991, when Dublin was quite a sleepy city and the sight of anyone rushing was remarkable. Elise wondered what the emergency was. A few minutes later she entered the park and saw this man again. He was sitting on a bench, in a particularly lovely spot, quietly eating his lunch and reading his newspaper. He had been rushing to relax. He had been rushing to get *that seat*.

Like this man, many people believe that being peaceful requires finding somewhere especially peaceful or beautiful— a perfect place. This is a common misunderstanding. We believe that we can only be peaceful when we're away from the kids, out of the city, on a deserted island, or on that perfect park bench. Yes, it's true that peaceful environments can help us to be peaceful. But it's also true that peaceful people spread peace wherever they are, and that it's possible to be peaceful anywhere. So it's okay to try the Basic Minute in an environment that you wouldn't normally associate with peacefulness, for example . . .

At work

Each day, when you arrive at work, you do many small rituals, such as turning on your computer, pouring a cup of coffee, opening your mail, and watering the plant. Think of the Basic Minute as another one of these. If you have a private office, it should be very easy to start your day with a Basic Minute. You can also do a Basic Minute at lunchtime to mark the half-way point of the day. Or you can do a Basic Minute at the end of the day to help you leave work at work.

If you don't have your own office, try doing a Minute in a storeroom or empty conference room. If that's not possible, then I recommend going to the bathroom. Yes, really. Many people already go to the bathroom when they need a break and can't justify it any other way. And many people grab a few extra minutes while they're in there. Sitting on the toilet seems to be one of the few activities for which we still insist on solitude, and about which no one asks any questions. So by all means, try a Basic Minute while sitting on the toilet. (You might want to make a special trip for this purpose.)

In the car

You can also try the Basic Minute in your car—before you start the engine, or while you're waiting for the engine to warm up. Or slip off the road secretly on your way to work or an appointment. Of course, it's possible that a security guard will get suspicious, seeing you sitting there doing nothing, or that a Good Samaritan will come over to make sure you're okay. Just say that everything's fine—you just needed a Minute.

> Please consider now where and when you might
> do the Basic Minute. Choose a timeplace that
> is realistic and that you can use every day.
> Look for gaps in your schedule that already
> exist, or that could be opened up just a little
> bit more. Then try the Basic Minute there.

The Benefits (for you)

I f you practice the Basic Minute regularly, you will begin to notice that there are many minutes throughout your day in which you could, in theory, take a Minute, no matter how busy you are. Just noticing these opportunities will change your relationship to time, because in noticing them, your mind is pausing, ever so slightly, instead of charging ahead mindlessly.

As you keep practicing the Basic Minute, you will find that you are "dropping into it" more quickly and deeply. You will find it easier to detach yourself from your everyday concerns, and become absorbed, briefly, in your breathing. You will begin to taste what could be called "stillness" or "peacefulness." But these are just words for what is actually indescribable—something beyond the reach of words. In the Basic Minute, all words and wording cease. It's hard to imagine all the benefits that can result from taking this time out of time (even for such a short time). Some will become clearer as we go. In this chapter, I'll just mention a few.

•   •   •

The most obvious benefit of the Basic Minute is that it can help you reduce stress, instantly. Stress is implicated in so many medical conditions—particularly high blood pressure and problems with the immune system. In the Basic Minute, your thinking mellows, your emotions become less turbulent, your breathing becomes deeper and slower, and your heart rate should drop a bit, too. Although you are sitting up, you are also unwinding. This may not relieve all your stress right away, but it *is* a start. For many people, taking just one minute off in this way can be a radical change. Each time you do a Minute you are also sending a signal—first of all, to yourself—that you are at least sometimes willing to stop. And that's just for starters.

The Basic Minute can also help you to become more "emotionally intelligent." In his book, *Emotional Intelligence,* Daniel Goleman has demonstrated that emotional intelligence is even more important to professional success than "mental intelligence" or IQ. A person who is emotionally intelligent has the ability to notice and respect his own feelings and the feelings of others, and he can also rise above his feelings— or at least take time out from them—when necessary. In Part 2, we will look at adaptations of the Basic Minute that you can use in emotionally charged situations. But for now, let's just say that the Basic Minute helps you get a grip on yourself when you're out of control, catch up with yourself when you're speeding, and find yourself when you're lost.

With the Basic Minute you can also learn to get beyond whatever is habitual or mechanical about your thinking. You can unhook yourself from whatever you think or believe unconsciously: it's like a break from the prison of your perceptions. If you want to taste freedom, this is it. Of course, once you are free, you are free to choose to believe or to think whatever you like. You are free to affirm whatever really matters to you—but as you no longer feel compelled, your choices are more genuine.

The Basic Minute also helps you learn to focus and concentrate: it shapes and tones your mind. With the Minute, you are choosing to bring your mind to something you have chosen (in this case, your breathing). Once you know how to do that, you can put your mind to anything.

The Basic Minute can also help with time management. You learn to notice when you're not working efficiently and you find more opportunities for a break. You also have something to do in that break that is not wasting time but restoring time. (The Basic Minute is profoundly unproductive.) As you will see later, this can radically change your perception of busyness—and of time itself. Time simply becomes less of a problem, because you have found more space in it.

The Basic Minute also helps you to live in a more conscious way. When you are able to take a break from your habitual self, you are less likely to do things impulsively or compulsively. You are less likely to buy what you don't need, say what you don't mean, or get involved with activities you're not passionate about. You are less likely to follow the crowd.

The Basic Minute also helps you make decisions better. You can clear your mind at will, giving you the chance to find new ideas, to hear other points-of-view, or clarify your values and goals. The Basic Minute also helps you avoid minor mishaps, and even serious accidents, because you begin to notice when you are stressed or off-balance, and have a way to right yourself.

Perhaps the greatest benefit of the Basic Minute is the simplest: it gives you a chance to refresh your awareness. After a whole day, not to mention a whole life, your mind is liable to be a bit cluttered. Just as your computer, your home, and your body all need maintenance to function well, so does your mind. And with just one minute a day, you can de-bug and de-fragment your mind, improving its performance significantly. You can remove the limiting perspectives of the past and see the limitless possibilities of the present.

•   •   •

The greatest challenge you will face, at this stage, is believing that something so simple and short can have so many benefits. But the more you believe in the Basic Minute, and apply yourself to it with enthusiasm, the more benefits it will give you. Just keep doing the Basic Minute, faithfully, once a day, and you will see how its benefits—though small at first—seem to deepen and multiply. Little by little, the Minutes start to resonate with one another, and then amplify one another, until peacefulness becomes the soundtrack of your life.

Please do a Basic Minute now.

The Benefits
(for everyone else)

Practicing the Basic Minute is not just good for you—it's good for other people also. It can even be considered an act of altruism. When you practice the Basic Minute, people around you will experience you as calmer, more patient, less likely to jump at them, and less likely to jump to conclusions. You are more likely to know what you really want to be doing, so you are less likely to create chaos by doing something else, and you are less likely to act impulsively. You are more likely to act clearly and decisively, on a firmer foundation, and not just for the sake of seeming decisive. You have better ideas and come up with better suggestions because you can see things more clearly. You are more available to help because you are more available. In other words, instead of creating confusion, you create calmness. Perhaps most importantly, you see people for who they are and accept them for who they are. You see others more clearly because, every day, you take a Minute to wipe clean your own lenses.

When you practice the Basic Minute regularly, all these benefits will appear without you making any special effort.

People around you will simply start to notice them happening. They will start to remark on them and thank you for doing things that you didn't even know you were doing. They'll say things like: it's nice to have you around; you have a helpful presence; we want you on our team.

You might also want to tell people that you are practicing the One-Moment Method, so they can help you stay on track. Then, whenever you seem stressed or off-center, they can just say, 'I think you need a Minute here.'

Please try a Basic Minute now.

Common Challenges

When you first decide to carve out a minute of your day for the Minute, you may suddenly discover lots of reasons not to. This is because your normal way of being may be so threatened by this radical new adventure that it tries to stop you. Psychologists call this "resistance" and you may well experience some of it. Resistance usually manifests as an onslaught of seemingly good reasons *not* to do what you really want or need to do. It seems that just when we're on the verge of peace, all hell breaks loose.

One of the most common "reasons" people have for not taking a break is that they are too busy. Well, I hope that no one is really too busy for one minute a day. The whole point of the Basic Minute is that it gives you some of the advantages of a much longer break in just a minute. But if you still feel that even one minute, once a day, is too much time for you, take heart: in future exercises, you'll learn how to get the same benefits in even less time. But you do have to start with the Minute.

Another common resistance is embarrassment. Some people find it hard to say to their boss or their employees or their friends or their children "I just need a Minute here," as if it were a sign of weakness. If that's you, well then by all means do your Minute clandestinely. But some day, when you're ready, consider coming out as a Basic Minute practitioner. Consider saying publicly that, from time to time, you need some time. You might find that there are some other people out there like you.

Sometimes resistance takes the form of grandiosity, which goes something like this: "The world won't survive if I take a Minute" or "I'm too important here to take a Minute." This is probably true if, for example, you are piloting a plane on your own. But in most other cases, it's absurd. Indeed, the opposite is probably true: if you really believe that you are so vital to what is happening around you that you can't afford a Minute, it's a very good indication that you need a Minute desperately, and that everyone else needs you to take one, too.

Another common resistance is guilt. Many people feel guilty for withdrawing their attention from the world, as if this were a selfish act. Isn't it strange that we rarely feel selfish for going on expensive vacations, or buying big cars or big televisions, but we do feel selfish when we want a tiny bit of time for ourselves—one minute a day in which to do nothing? If you suffer from this belief, try to remember what I said before—that the Minute is actually an act of altruism. Not only are you helping other people by becoming peaceful, you are also modeling good behavior. Part of Basic Training is to learn that peace of mind deserves at least a minute of your time.

You may also encounter some practical challenges in doing the Minute. The first is that you can't find somewhere quiet enough. Let's face it: nowhere is absolutely silent. And if your mind wants to find something to distract you, it will. But it's sufficient to *try* to find a quiet place—so please don't get obsessed about finding somewhere completely silent. Accept the noise around you and just try not to focus on it. Learn how to rest your attention in your breath in spite of the sound around.

My friend Randy Hostetler was a composer who noticed and enjoyed every sound he heard around him. He recorded the sounds of the world—the unique tones of car engines revving, hinges squeaking, and floors creaking—and he mixed these together in his compositions. As his grandmother said, Randy "never heard noise, he heard only music." In this respect, Randy was a master.

The most important thing to arrange is that you will not be interrupted by someone who is specifically looking for you. However if you *are* interrupted, try not to be angry. Eventually, some day, you will be uninterruptible. (You will be uninterruptible because you will be imperturbable.) In the meantime, if you do get interrupted and have to stop your Minute, just yield the rest of that Minute over to whatever it is. Accept what is happening graciously, open your eyes, and keep breathing.

Another common challenge is fatigue, because so many of us are sleep deprived. We are so "on the go" that when we stop, we fall asleep. But although the Basic Minute can be relaxing, it's not meant to be *that* relaxing. It's really about a kind of relaxed alertness, a feeling of peaceful awakeness that is *very* different from sleep. So try to stay awake for the Basic

Minute. If you can't do that, then you probably need a nap, or an earlier bedtime.

You might also, at times, have trouble staying present in your breath. Your mind will be filled with doubts, distractions, mental noise, negative thinking, and plans, and you simply can't let go of these, even for a minute. But even then, there is still great benefit in just sitting there—in having some time, each day, to sit in this posture and be still.

Think of it this way: If you were floating down a river on a raft, you might become so entranced by the scenery—the trees on the riverbank, or the clouds in the sky—that you would forget you're on a raft. But you would still be on that raft, and every so often you would remember—perhaps with a jolt— "I'm on a raft!" So even though you may think that the Basic Minute isn't working, you are still sitting there each day, sitting still. And one day you will realize—perhaps with a jolt— that you're more peaceful than you were before.

You may also discover that some unfamiliar aspects of yourself come to the surface while you're doing a Minute. Whenever you separate yourself from your ordinary concerns, there is some room for deeper issues to emerge into your awareness—thoughts and feelings that you have repressed, forgotten, or never even knew about. They are emerging so that you can be free of them. This is your mind's way of cleaning out the basement, so to speak, now that it has the chance. While this might be temporarily disruptive, in the long run you'll have a lot more space.

You may also find that, during the Basic Minute, you experience an upsurge of small aches and pains. If you are sitting correctly, these aches and pains are not being caused by your sitting. More likely, they are little repressed aches and pains, leftover feelings from old injuries, or just chronic stress, coming up to be released.

Finally, you may find that in spite of your commitment and enthusiasm, when you sit down to do the Basic Minute, you find yourself not wanting to be here. This might take the form of pleasant fantasies about other places you would rather be—in bed, on the beach, in the bar—or it could take the form of a very strong desire to be *anywhere but here*. Unavoidably, there is something about the Basic Minute that really pins you down, and no one likes to be pinned down. We like to keep our options open. We all want wiggle room. The Basic Minute may be the first time in your life that you are actually trying to be in one place at one time: mind, body, heart and soul. This is an important ability to have, because if we don't know how to be in one place at one time, we will always be fragmented. If you really want to experience peace of mind, you must learn to be peaceful wherever you are. So consider the Minute a short but valuable way for you to learn how to be where you are, even if you don't like it sometimes.

Please do a Basic Minute now.

The Warm-Up

If you would like to double the effectiveness of the Basic Minute, and can find just *half* a minute more to spare, this chapter is for you.

Whenever we want to perform at our peak, warming up is essential. Actors, dancers, musicians, public speakers and athletes all take their warm-up very seriously, and we all prepare for meetings and cram for exams. A warm-up to the Basic Minute is helpful because, without it, the transition from your ordinary, stressful mind to a Basic Minute can feel a bit sudden. Without a warm-up, you might well spend most of the Basic Minute just arriving in the Basic Minute.

A warm-up is also a symbolic act, a ritual of preparation, in which you reinforce the importance of what you're about to do and remind yourself that you take it seriously. A ritual involves clearing a space for something powerful to happen, and in making this space, you improve your chances of success. Imagine an artist assembling his brushes or a surgeon scrubbing her hands: these acts are not just functional, they also prepare the mind.

To warm up for the Basic Minute, here are some suggestions. Do some simple stretching exercises, or shake out any tension in your arms and legs. Jump around a bit. Make some noise. Take one or two very deep breaths. Yawn. Sigh. Wash your hands and face. Light a candle. Write down a thought that you've been obsessing about and then tear up the paper. Name a decision that you need help with, and then forget about it. Dedicate your upcoming Basic Minute to someone you love, or to someone who needs help or healing. One of my favorite warm-ups is simply to clean what's right in front of me. I don't get too involved or make it a big project—I just stack some papers or return a paperclip to its place.

Experiment with any of these techniques that appeal to you, or make up one of your own, but once you find one that works, please stick with it. Make it habitual. Then the simple act of beginning the ritual will put your mind in a deeper, calmer place. But don't let this ritual get *too* habitual either. Although the warm-up must feel familiar, it must also feel fresh. So keep it fresh by varying it from time to time. And by all means, pay as much attention to the warm-up as you do to the Minute: it's never too early to be here.

**Try doing a Basic Minute with
a warm-up right now.**

**In the coming week, try a different warm-up
each day until you find the one you like
best. Then make that warm-up your regular
introduction to the Basic Minute.**

The Cool-Down

You can add even more value to the Basic Minute by taking time afterwards for a short cool-down—a ritual of completion. The purpose of this cool-down is to help you to consolidate the benefits of the Minute just past. It gives you a softer landing, helping you to come back to your normal state gently—so it's not too much of a shock.

This consolidation period also helps you to marry the experience of the Minute with the experience of the rest of your life. If you didn't do a cool-down, you might think that life is either one thing or the other: peace or stress. But with the cool-down, you make a gradual transition to ordinary concerns while still feeling the immediate benefits of the Minute. The cool-down helps you notice your "habitual mind," or how you function in the world: What is your tipping point from peacefulness to stress? What is the first thing that bothers you? What knocks you off balance?

For the cool-down, you can try any of the warm-up techniques from the last chapter, or you can try any one of these specific cool-down techniques:

- Wiggle your toes.
- Tap your feet on the floor.
- Look around slowly.
- Notice your first impulse.
- Look out the window.
- Consider how the Minute was for you. Was it pleasant? Difficult?
- Pat yourself on the back for a Minute well done.

Try a Basic Minute now, with a cool-down.
Then try a Basic Minute with a
warm-up and a cool-down.

In the coming week, experiment with different
cool-downs until you find the one you like best.
Then add this to your Basic Minute every day.

Practice and Perfection

Most spiritual traditions have, as their aim, some kind of "ultimate" experience. With some subtle variations, that experience has been called enlightenment, grace, or surrender. Storyteller Spalding Gray called it the "perfect moment." While this is a wonderful goal, the reality is that most of the time your Minutes will feel far from perfect. You'll be painfully aware of every distraction, and maybe even feel that you've failed. That's why spiritual traditions teach us that effort—even vigilance—is required. They say that we must practice (or pray or surrender) a lot in order to achieve perfection. On the other hand, most people who have experienced a perfect moment say that, once experienced, it must still be practiced—otherwise it is lost or forgotten. So although practice makes perfect, perfection must also be practiced. Either way, practice is the key.

With practice, you will find that you "click in" to your Minute more quickly. You will find that just by getting into the *form* of a Minute—doing the warm-up, sitting in the chair, adopting the posture—you become more peaceful. The Basic Minute becomes an old, faithful friend that you look forward to seeing each day. Some day you might even be able to benefit from a Minute just by *imagining* one. No matter where you are, the Basic Minute becomes like home.

But there is another benefit of regular, dedicated practice. With the Basic Minute, you are creating a new psychological space for yourself, and each time you practice the Minute, you are going a little bit further into that space. In this, you are like the scout for a mountaineering group who climbs up ahead of the others to check the terrain, clear a trail, and set up camp. Then she comes back down the mountain and says: "Yes, it's there. I know the way. And the rest of you can get there, too." Each time you practice the Basic Minute, you are like this scout—going just a little bit further on behalf of the rest of you. Each time you come back from the Basic Minute, you are reminding the rest of you that "a place of calm and focus exists, and in time, we will all live there." Indeed, that's exactly what happens: in time, your whole life is lived from this new place and you see everything from a new point-of-view.

Please do a Basic Minute now.
Don't worry if it isn't "perfect."

The Minute
and Prayer

The Basic Minute shouldn't be confused with prayer. The word "prayer" comes from the Latin word "to entreat," and it means "an address to a god or spiritual power in the form of a petition."[2] But in the Basic Minute, there is no thought of anyone outside yourself to petition—there is only the breath. The purpose of the Basic Minute is for you to experience *just being*—not to think about anything, and not to talk to anyone, not even God.

That said, doing the Basic Minute and praying are complementary practices. So you can certainly say a prayer before doing the Basic Minute. You can also dedicate or offer your Minute to something greater than you: your guardian angel, your patron saint, all beings, or God.

In its deepest sense, prayer is an expression of gratitude and a way to align yourself with what is greater than you. This attitude of humility, however, is not always so easy to adopt. If you do a Basic Minute before praying, this might help you to empty your mind, let go of any thoughts of personal gain, and become truly still and centered. With the Basic Minute, you are cleaning your mind as you might clean a temple. You are creating a sacred space in which to pray with all your heart.

Try doing a Basic Minute with a prayer just before it or a prayer just after it.

Potential Side Effects

As you practice the Basic Minute, you may encounter two significant side effects: bliss and compassion. This chapter explains how to cope with them.

Not everyone will experience bliss in a Basic Minute. It's not really part of the plan. But if you do experience bliss, it's okay to enjoy it. The experience of bliss can tickle you in places you didn't even know you had. But do be careful, for like any pleasure, bliss can become addictive. You can find yourself craving it when it's gone, and this just increases your suffering, because ordinary life—without bliss—can just seem so, well, ordinary. The best strategy is just to enjoy bliss when it appears—like a new color added to your palette—but by all means let it go easily when it leaves. Return to just being.

Another common side effect of the Minute is that you begin to feel more deeply moved by other people's problems. It's a curious paradox: as you become more able to sit with yourself, you begin to care more deeply about everybody else. It's not that you feel compelled to fix their problems for them—it's just that you care more. This is called *compassion*, which means "suffering with."

Compassion is a natural, unavoidable consequence of being more peaceful within yourself. As you begin to quiet your mind and take a break from your own thoughts, you begin to make contact with a part of you that is more universal. You just feel more connected to everyone else. You feel what they feel as if you were feeling it. And you are more able to see things from their point of view.

But compassion is not just a *result* of peacefulness—it is also a *cause* of peacefulness. The more we feel for others, the less likely we are to think in terms of harming or being harmed. When you feel compassion, you are more peaceful because you perceive that no one is fundamentally different from you. It goes like this: less fear, more peace.

Please make sure that you're comfortable with the Minute, and have practiced it for at least a month, before moving on to Part 2. For if you are not truly grounded in a minute, you will surely lose your head in a moment.

PART 2
Intermediate Training

The Portable Minute

Now that you are comfortable with the Basic Minute, it's time to try the Portable Minute. The Portable Minute will enable you to bring the Basic Minute with you wherever you go, and do it in all sorts of awkward situations. It's also an essential transition to mastering the moment.

Before you can practice the Portable Minute, however, you must do a little research. Fortunately, this won't take any time at all. It's just a slight change in your Basic Minute. Here's how to do it:

The next time you do the Basic Minute, instead of simply focusing on your breath, *count* each breath. Count the first inhalation as "one," the first exhalation as "two," the second inhalation as "three," and so on. When the alarm sounds, note your count. If you lose track, don't worry. Just try again another day. Do this for several days until you have several counts, and then average them. This is your average one-minute *breathcount*—the number of breaths you take in a typical relaxed minute.

Once you have this average breathcount, you can do the Basic Minute without the timer. You simply do a warm-up, close your eyes, and then—with full attention—count your breaths . . . just up to your breathcount. Then open your eyes and do a cool-down.

This is a liberation of no small significance. You deserve the heartiest of congratulations for now . . . you can put away your timer. (Note that you are not yet free of time, just free of the timer.) You are able to take the Portable Minute with you anywhere, and use it in all sorts of places where setting an alarm might be inappropriate: trains, airplanes, restaurants, libraries, theaters, at your desk, at the gym, in the shower, nursing your baby, and even in bed with someone sleeping next to you. You can do it while waiting for the deal to close, the show to start, the jury to decide.

Do make sure to do the breathcount all the way to the end. For example, if your breathcount is twenty-six, resist the temptation to say, "Well, I've made it to twenty-four, that's good enough. Might as well stop now." The little bit at the end is often the most valuable, and surprising, part of the Minute.

The Portable Minute, of course, is not quite as precise as the Basic Minute, because the rate of your breathing does vary from time to time. When you're stressed or anxious, breathing tends to be quicker, so your breathcount might last less than a minute. When you're relaxed, breathing tends to be slower, so your breathcount might last somewhat more than a minute. In other words, the Portable Minute is really an approximate minute, but that's okay. The benefits of portability outweigh the costs of imprecision.

Every so often, check your breathcount against a timer to see if it has changed, and revise it accordingly, so that you are still doing approximately one minute. Over time, you may find that it takes fewer and fewer breaths to reach a minute—that your breathing is getting slower. You may wonder where all this is heading. You may wonder just how slow you can go. But try not to panic. It just means you are becoming more and more relaxed. It's just the way you are.

Over several days, find your average one-minute breathcount. Practice the Portable Minute once a day (or more) for one week before reading further.

The Emergency Minute

Have you ever wanted to hit the pause button on your life? Have you ever reacted impulsively to a situation, knowing full well that what you were saying or doing was not really what you wanted to be saying or doing? Have you ever wanted to shout: "Give me a minute to hear myself think" or "Give me a minute to get my head together"?

The good news is that we each have a general-purpose first-aid kit for these situations. It's called the Emergency Minute, and it's simply a Portable Minute that is available in a crisis— exactly when we need it most.

But if you really want to have an Emergency Minute ready when necessary, you must practice the Portable Minute on a regular basis. In this regard, your training is just like that of any other emergency worker. Just like fire-fighters, police officers, and paramedics, you have to learn the skills *and* you have to do the drills, so that in a time of crisis, you are READY. Then you'll be able to do a Minute even in a difficult, chaotic situation. Even more importantly, you'll *remember* to do it.

There are actually just two kinds of emergencies: the kind in which you know what to do right away, and all the other kinds. In a real life-and-death emergency—when you must catch something before it falls or run through the flames to save a child—there's really no need for an Emergency Minute because you react instantly, without thinking. The Emergency Minute is really for all those other situations in life when you *think* you have to act urgently but don't *really* have to. With the Emergency Minute, you will be less likely to react out of panic or confusion or anger, and less likely to make things worse.

Here are some specific situations in which the Emergency Minute can come in handy, with some minor adaptations for each situation:

Panic

When we feel panicked, our breathing becomes fast and shallow, and seems to have a mind of its own. Unfortunately, this becomes a vicious cycle: the more we panic, the shallower and faster our breathing becomes; the shallower and faster our breathing becomes, the more we panic. In this case, it may not be sufficient just to count your breaths; you must consciously try to slow your breathing. It's like doing a Portable Minute with the brakes on. You might also need to do this exercise more than once, but if so, keep each time distinct. Take a short break after each one to reassess the situation, and then, if you need to, do another Minute.

Anger

When you feel a sudden surge of anger, it is very hard to remember your normal way of looking at things. It's hard to look at things rationally, see the bigger picture, or see someone else's point of view. Now there is nothing wrong with anger *per se*; it's a normal human emotion and it can bring great benefits. The problem is when anger is out of control, when it won't let go, or when it does some real harm to others.

The classic strategy for coping with anger is "counting to ten." If you count to ten, the theory goes, you won't erupt. It's a nice idea, but for me, when I'm angry and count to ten, it just feels like I'm biding time. I resent every single count and am just waiting until ten to be angry again. In other words, counting to ten may delay your outburst, but it doesn't do a lot to transform your anger.

But an Emergency Minute is something else entirely. The difference is that in an Emergency Minute, you return to an experience that is deeply familiar. That "place" within yourself that you found with the Basic Minute is like a refuge that you carry with you everywhere. And the more you have practiced the Basic Minute and the Portable Minute, the easier it is to find that place.

Imagine a rodeo cowboy, sitting on an angry bull that is being held back in his pen. As the bull is released into the ring, bucking furiously, the cowboy's only task is to *stay on*. The cowboy is not trying to stop the bull, pacify the bull, bring the bull back into the pen, make friends with the bull, or effect a religious conversion of the bull. *Just stay on.* So too with your anger. Try not to be thrown off by it or be flung into the air. Feel the energy that has been released from its pen and breathe with it. Trying to force an angry bull to calm down, before he's ready, will only make him angrier or more panicked. In other words, don't treat the energy of anger as a bad thing that you must resist. *Just breathe with it.* You may even discover that, once things settle down a bit, the experience has been very energizing.

Pressure

The Emergency Minute can also be useful when you're under pressure. You might experience this pressure coming at you from outside—from work, your partner, your children—and feel that you will *implode.* Or you might experience it coming at you from inside—a great build-up of frustration at everything—and you feel like you will *explode.*

In these cases, just imagining that you're free of pressure isn't very helpful. As with anger, it's important to honor the energy as it is. A helpful image here is a pressure cooker. A pressure cooker uses intense pressure in order to cook food slowly, but it also lets off steam, a little at a time, so that it doesn't explode. So as you do an Emergency Minute under pressure, try lengthening your out-breath, ever so slightly, as if you were a pressure cooker. It's even helpful to make a little sound as you exhale, like a whistle. But don't release too much too soon. When you're under pressure, it often feels better to release that pressure slowly rather than quickly, for you may actually need some of it: there may be something cooking inside you. So just like a pressure cooker, release just a little steam at a time; this will ensure that you keep cooking, but don't blow.

Confusion

We all have moments in which we feel intensely confused about an important decision—when we really need an answer *right now* but the answer, despite our best efforts, just isn't available. Personally, I believe that if the answer isn't obvious, then it isn't *ready* to be obvious. The Emergency Minute is helpful because you have no choice in this situation but to wait, and the Emergency Minute is the best possible thing you can do while waiting. First of all, it gives you a rest from the confusion—some breathing space. Second, you will be more likely to be ready for the answer when it appears. Third, because your mind is clearer, there is a greater chance that you'll notice the answer when it *does* appear. Finally, the Emergency Minute helps you to be more accepting of the fact that—right now, at least—you *just don't know,* and it helps prevent you from acting, in the meantime, out of desperation.

Shock

Animals, in an emergency, are said to exhibit one of two responses: fight or flight. But this is not the whole range of animal responses. Another typical response for animals is to *play dead.* Psychiatrist Ivor Browne has observed that many humans do something similar in traumatic situations.[3] Sometimes, when we are shocked or overwhelmed, our diaphragms freeze and our breathing becomes very shallow, part of what's called a "startle response." In other words, we shut down, emotionally and physically, as if dead. And it can take a long time—sometimes years or even a lifetime—to learn to breathe fully and become fully alive again.

Though playing dead may be a valuable coping mechanism in some situations—when we just can't bear to take in what is happening—it also inhibits our ability to process what is happening and make decisions. When you play dead, you cut yourself off from the flow of experience, and over time, become less able to experience anything. When you play dead, you are saying: "This isn't happening to me." But the fact is that it *is* happening to you.

If you do an Emergency Minute as soon as you are startled or shocked, then you stay present for the experience and stay connected to life. Whereas restricting the diaphragm says, "This isn't happening to me," liberating the diaphragm says, "This *is* happening to me and I can breathe through it." And as you breathe through it, you realize that you *are* breathing through it, that you're still here, and that you can cope.

•　•　•

No matter what is happening around you, the only thing that you can surely change is yourself. You may not be able to avert an economic downturn or a natural disaster. You may not be able to finish your work on time. You may not be able to make other people do what you want them to do. But you *can* take a minute off. You can take a minute to stop the speeding car of your life—and wipe the windshield. You can take a one-minute vacation by vacating your mind of all its concerns. You can take a one-minute holiday by touching something in yourself that feels holy.

Take a minute now to write down some situations in which you have experienced (or tend to experience) anger, confusion, panic, pressure, or shock—those times when you could use an Emergency Minute.

As you read the following chapters, keep practicing the Portable Minute once a day, and the Emergency Minute as needed.

The Surprise Minute

Once you have mastered the Basic Minute, and liberated yourself with the Portable Minute, you can try the Surprise Minute. Surprise Minutes, by definition, are not planned, so they can't be practiced. They happen like this: First you realize that there is nothing that you absolutely *have* to do right now. Then you start to notice a little pull toward peacefulness, a little craving to have just a little minute for yourself. Finally, you say, "What the heck, I'm going to take a Minute." Surprise!

They are quite delightful, these Surprise Minutes—real boons in a busy life, and the more you have practiced the Basic Minute and the Portable Minute, the more Surprise Minutes you will find throughout your day. You will actually be surprised to discover how many Surprise Minutes there are, even in days you thought were quite busy. These Surprise Minutes have always been there, but you didn't notice them. Or perhaps you noticed them, but didn't have anything particularly useful to do with them. Now you know differently. You see that each day has many, many opportunities to grab a Minute.

Each time you grab a Surprise Minute—especially when you *don't* need one—you are also making it just a little bit less likely that you will become stressed or conflicted later. It's a pre-emptive strike for peace.

As you find more and more Surprise Minutes in your day, you may discover that you're not nearly as busy as you thought. Many of the things that you thought you had to do, you don't have to do. Many of the things you used to do in a distracted or complicated way now happen more easily and take less time. And many of the things you used to want to do aren't half as enjoyable as doing a Minute. You may also discover that even when you *are* busy, you don't *feel* busy: you handle everything with equanimity, one thing flowing into the next. Now you're really getting somewhere.

Do a Surprise Minute right now.

The Bonus Minute

One of the great hopes we had for technology was that it would give us more time. Things haven't worked out that way. It seems that whenever a new device comes along to help us save time, we fill that time with more activity. We move faster and faster, do more and more, and though generally richer than ever before in history, we feel "time poor."

One reason for this, I suspect, is that although technology saves us time, it takes away mental space. Back when we had to do more tasks by hand, these tasks took longer to do, and while we did them, we had more time to think, daydream, or not-think. So as we spend less time doing simple manual jobs, our minds get less time off.

The Bonus Minute provides a way to compensate for this. It actually enhances the time-saving benefits of technology. Here's how you do it: Whenever you notice that something has taken less time than you thought it would, take a Minute to celebrate. Whenever you arrive somewhere earlier than expected, or you finish something before the deadline, take a Minute in gratitude. When your computer crashes and you are getting ready to spend an infuriating hour on the phone with tech support, but then, to your surprise, you get connected quickly to a friendly person who fixes the problem in fifteen minutes, think: "I've just saved forty-five minutes. Surely I can use one of those minutes for a Minute."

As you become more accustomed to this practice, take a Bonus Minute whenever you notice that what you're doing would have taken a lot longer to do fifty or one hundred years ago. So when you're travelling by plane, realize how much longer the journey would have been by boat, and take a Minute. When you send an email, realize how much longer it would have taken to write that letter by hand, and take a Minute. When you put your clothes in the washing machine, realize how much longer it would have taken you to scrub those clothes against a rock in the river, and take a Minute.

The Bonus Minute gives you a way to reinvest the dividends of technology in the bank of well-being. This is really the only way to save time.

Experiment with the Emergency Minute,
the Surprise Minute, and the Bonus Minute
whenever the opportunity presents itself
to you. Meanwhile, practice the Portable
Minute once a day, for thirty days,
before trying the next exercises.

PART 3
The Moment in Time

As you practice the techniques in this book, you may find that you have more time, that time seems to expand, or just that you're thinking about time in a different way. That's because the One-Moment Method is intended to loosen up your experience of time, one moment at a time.

As this may be unsettling, or just hard to believe, I have written this more philosophical part of the book to show you that time is not as fixed a thing as we tend to think. This part of the book is for those of you who, like me, find that a little philosophizing can sometimes help to clear the mind. It helps to cut away some assumptions, leaving us more open to genuine experience. But feel free to skip Part 3 entirely, if you wish, for it's not really essential to the One-Moment Method. What counts most is your experience.

The Perception of Time

Although we tend to believe that time is a fixed thing "out there," the way we experience of time is actually quite variable. It depends on how we feel, what we're doing, how old we are, our cultural backgrounds, and even our place in history. In other words, although we think of time as *absolute*, our experience of time is *relative*.

When we're young, we have all the time in the world. We have so much time that we can't imagine it running out. We even yearn for time to pass more quickly. ("Six" seems *so* far away when you're "five-and-three-quarters.") Around the age of forty, however, we begin to feel that time is passing too quickly, and that we may never get the chance to do all those things we've been putting off. In later years, we become painfully aware that "our days are numbered." Even waking up each morning is not taken for granted. (My parents joke that, at their age, they don't even buy green bananas.) The great psychological challenge of old age is to make sense of the time we've had and make peace with the time we have left.

When we're enjoying ourselves, time seems to pass quickly. ("Time flies when you're having fun.") But when we're bored or waiting anxiously, we become hyper-aware of time and it seems to pass slowly. ("A watched pot never boils.")

One of the most rewarding experiences of time is actually a non-experience of time called a "flow state." According to psychologist Mihaly Csikszentmihalyi, this state occurs when we are intensely engaged in an activity that is challenging but not too challenging. In a flow state we actually *stop noticing time*. We have the paradoxical experience of time passing quickly—because we're enjoying ourselves so much—but also of having plenty of time—because we are so attentive to what we're doing.

Sometimes time is experienced as enabling and helpful. For example, when we are recovering from an illness, we believe that time is the "great healer," and when we are grieving, friends advise us to "give it time." But when we are depressed, time does not seem to be "on our side." We lose our faith in the flow of time, as if the movie of life had frozen on a particularly unpleasant frame. When the depression lifts, however, time starts to move again: we remember that all things pass and we believe that life will get better when they do.

Attitudes toward time also vary from culture to culture. In some cultures, people don't rush, while in others, people don't know how to slow down. In some cultures, time is approximate, while in others, time is exact. I once coordinated a project involving both Irish people and Japanese people where this difference became a real problem. After several days of confusion about meeting times, my Japanese colleagues asked me, with some exasperation, to clarify whether the schedule was in

"Japanese time" or "Irish time": Japanese time was always right on the dot; Irish time was always give or take a half hour.

We each pass different judgments about time, too. Some people believe that being busy is a sign of success or popularity. Some people do everything possible to "keep busy," afraid of what they might feel if they weren't. Some people consider keeping busy a virtue in itself, as if having free time were a sin. Other people, such as artists and writers, crave unlimited free time in order to create. Monks and nuns take months or even years for silent contemplation—and consider this time sacred.

Our perception of time is also all wound up with work. In the Industrial Age—with mechanical clocks, assembly lines, and efficiency studies—it became important to know precisely how many units got produced in any given period of time and exactly when each worker punched the clock. In general, the longer you worked, the more you got paid. No wonder we came to believe that time was money. No wonder we started watching the clock. And counting. And counting. And counting.

In the Information Age, we are moving toward "flexible time." Time-based work doesn't make as much sense as it once did, as ideas are not "things" and can't be measured in units. An idea, conceived in just a moment, can have enormous implications. Thus an "idea person" has a more flexible approach to time. She learns how to develop the special, and often quite eccentric, circumstances that encourage creativity, and to trust inspiration when it appears—no matter what the time.

Technology has also altered our sense of time. Nowadays, we live "above" nature, as if we have mastered its rhythms. Fruits and vegetables that were once only seasonal are now available, shrink-wrapped, all year round. We are no longer bound by the sun: with electric lighting, central heating, air conditioning and the Internet, our world is open for business . . . and pleasure . . . 24/7. We can now do whatever we want, right through the dormant days of winter and blazing heat of summer. In cities and suburbs, we consider snow and rain to be interruptions: nature is something that messes up our commute.

Back when travel was on horseback and we didn't have phones, our experience of time must have been more approximate. It must have been commonplace to arrive days or even weeks late after a long journey. These days, however, we micro-manage time. We check arrival and departure information online and on our phones. And we narrate each stage of the journey: "I'm stuck in traffic. I'm just stopping for gas. I'm on the train. I'm getting off the train. I'm five minutes away. Meet me downstairs in a minute. I'm at the door." But as we account for time more and more precisely, we also make ourselves just that little bit crazier. We become jealous of time, obsessed with time, guarded about time. And it seems that the more precisely we count time, the less of it we have.

Some people, in order to do their job well, actually need less time: they need a deadline. The word "deadline" originally meant an actual line around a military prison, beyond which a prisoner was liable to be shot. Indeed that's how we often feel when we approach a deadline: as if we're going to die. Yet having the sense that time is "running out" seems to focus our minds on doing the last, most difficult, piece of work. A deadline can bring out that extra bit of enthusiasm, as if we were in a last dash to the finish line. There are many people who, without a deadline, would produce nothing at all; but given the pressure of a deadline, can make a diamond.

No matter what our perception of time, we are still physical creatures: we still have bodies that are subject to time, and in the back of our minds is the notion of time as the Bogeyman. For example, when women say that their "biological clock is ticking," it's never said with pleasure—only dread. Kindly old Father Time gets all mixed up with the Grim Reaper.

One of the most common perceptions of time is that it is a "prison." We feel shackled by time. We feel victimized—having too much to do and not enough time to do it. Working longer hours each day, and taking fewer days off, many people crave *more time* or at least some *time off*. With our lives so intensely scheduled, we lack opportunities in which to let go of time (or be let off its hook). We feel guilty about the lack of time we spend with our children, and try to console ourselves by saying it's not the *quantity* but the *quality*. We are so dominated by the cultural organization of time that we are alienated from our own natural rhythms. One of the real pleasures of taking a vacation or sabbatical is that these out-of-the-ordinary periods of time allow us to experience time more freely. We can stay up past our bedtime or go to sleep when we're tired.

But perhaps what we really crave is not to have *more time* or to have *time off* but to feel *free of time*. We want to experience what life would be like outside of time. Many people turn to drugs or alcohol just to have this experience. But we also experience this in dreams, stories, and our imagination. In these realms, we are free of time and space. (The opening phrase of fairy tales—"once upon a time"—doesn't mean "a long time ago" but "in a world beyond time.") In dreams we can walk through walls, change shape, become trees and animals and other people, meet our ancestors, and feel ourselves to be without limits. We are released from the weight of gravity— a feeling that we have probably not had since floating in the womb. In dreams, theater, films, songs, stories, and poems, we escape from the prison of time and get a taste of what's possible beyond it.

The Nature of Time

Although our perception of time varies, we still tend to believe that time is an objective "thing" out there. But there's a lot we don't know about the nature of time, and a lot that we may never know. Concludes physicist Paul Davies, "To be perfectly honest, neither scientists nor philosophers really know what time is or why it exists."[4] Some physicists and philosophers actually argue that time doesn't exist at all.

The purpose of this chapter is neither to reveal the true nature of time, nor give you an exhaustive history of time, but to help loosen up your assumptions about time. For the nature of time is inseparable from the nature of mind. So if you change your mind, you experience time differently . . . and you might even change time, too.

● ● ●

Throughout history, there have been two main views of time: time as cyclical and time as linear. Most societies have believed some combination of these two.

In the cyclical view, life seems to repeat itself without any progress or development. There is evidence for this right before our eyes: the sun rises and sets and rises again, the moon waxes and wanes and waxes again, and each season returns, year after year.

In the linear view of time, time is experienced as a line, rather than a circle: if you keep going straight, you will never get back to where you started. We have evidence for linear time right before our eyes, too: we see plants and people growing and aging, in a predictable direction. For most people, "linear time" also suggests that time has a direction, and that that direction is forward. (Of course, if you're standing on an infinite line, it's impossible to tell which direction is forward—we just follow the crowd.)

When humans first began to count time, our methods were based simply on the cycles of the sun and moon. A day was the period between one sunrise (or sunset) and the next. A month was the period between one new moon (or full moon) and the next. And the solar year was the period from one winter solstice (or summer solstice) to the next.

Even when calendars were introduced, about 5000 years ago, and we could easily count cycles adding up in a linear way, we still believed that this progression was subsumed in larger cycles of creation and destruction. If there was any progress within a cycle, it was considered temporary. We experienced a universe of endless return.

Calendars were certainly an *attempt* to count time and order time, but they have never represented natural cycles exactly. Nature is not as orderly as we would like it to be. (For example, the earth's rotation, on which the measurement of days and years is based, is actually irregular.) Our calendar is as much the result of political and scientific compromise as it is an accurate or stable map of time.

The concept of a month, for example, was originally based on phases of the moon, and doesn't fit into calendars that are measured in days, for these are based on the observations of the sun. Each lunar month actually lasts about 29.5 solar days, but our "months" now contain 28, 29, 30 or 31 days, just so we can have twelve of them in a year. And even though a "year" and a "day" are both derived from our position relative to the sun, they don't match each other as much as we'd like. A year is composed (on average) of 365 days, 5 hours, 48 minutes, and 45.51 seconds. That's just not a nice, round, or consistent number, so we have to adjust the system with leap years and even, occasionally, leap seconds.

So let's remember that very little of what we now think of as "time" is completely consistent with nature. The history of time is really the story of people's attempts to impose some kind of mental or cultural order on a natural world that isn't as tidy or ordered as we'd like it to be.

The linear view of time got a very big boost with the writing of Genesis, which posited a beginning of the universe in a one-time creative act by God. This concept of time spread widely, with the success of both Christian and Islamic civilisations.[5] Gone was the sense that our world was but one of many cycles of creation and destruction. With a sense of a definite starting point, we also began to think about where we might be going. The past and the future took on a whole new dimension.

But even with a linear sense of time, our ability to tell time, and therefore our sense of time, was still, for a long time, approximate. Until relatively recently, we lacked sophisticated timekeeping devices and a coherent theory for how to tell or measure time.

It is interesting to try to imagine what life was like before clocks of any kind. How did we know what time it was? How did we know when a specific period of time had passed? Primitive timekeeping devices were not that helpful. Sundials, based on the casting of shadows, only work when the sun is shining, and require adjustments based on latitude. Some cultures used hourglasses or burned a stick of incense to mark out defined periods, but these devices could not "keep" time, over time.

It wasn't until the eleventh century that the use of geared timekeeping mechanisms became widespread in Europe. And it was not until the fourteenth century, with the building of clock towers throughout Europe, that some kind of common or standard time was available (and audible) to all. And it was only with the development of the pendulum, in the seventeenth century, that the telling of time could be called even remotely accurate. Before the use of pendulums, clocks had a margin of error of +/− fifteen minutes per day. With the use of pendulums, this was reduced to +/− fifteen seconds.

The next big leap forward in time came at the end of the seventeenth century, with the physics of Isaac Newton. In Newton's view, space and time were like a container or grid in which everything else moved. Time passed without reference to anything else. Newton's laws required a universe in which space and time were absolute: invariable and taken for granted.

Newton used the mechanical clock as a metaphor for the universe itself, with God as the clockmaker who set the gears in motion, and the universe playing itself out according to His rules, like clockwork. (In employing this metaphor, Newton was perhaps influenced by a novelty of his time: the first pendulum clock had been produced only thirty years before.)

Newton's discoveries had enormous predictive power, and his ideas contributed strongly to both the scientific and industrial revolutions. His metaphor of a "clockwork universe" became the dominant understanding of time for over three hundred years. We came to see time as something fixed *out there*, as if there really were a giant clock, embedded in the universe, keeping time.

From Newton's mechanics came *mechanization*. Armed with the knowledge of matter and how it works, engineers were able to make dramatic changes to our world, and we came to believe that everything could be predictable and controllable, like a machine: if you put in *x*, then out comes *y* . . . and you know when to expect it. This certainly seemed to confirm our sense that the past caused the present, and the present causes the future. In other words, Newton's laws reinforced the linear view of time. And not only was linear progress possible: we could predict it.

Even so, it wasn't until the mid-nineteenth century that there was any way to know easily what time it was somewhere else. Remember that before the world was divided into time zones, all time was *extremely* local: time was based on where the sun was relative to *you*. This wasn't much of a problem until the invention of the electric telegraph and the growth of the railways started to speed things up. It became quite important to know, and yet very difficult to compute, the time at which people (and information) would arrive at their destination. With the World Exposition in London in 1851, and six million people travelling by train to London from all over Great Britain, the problem became acute—particularly for those people trying to write and read train timetables.

The solution was Greenwich Mean Time: an attempt to standardize time across Britain. Introduced in 1852, it was transmitted twice daily around the country by telegraph, informing everybody instantly of the *official* time—the time for the entire country. By 1884, in an extraordinary feat of global organization, the International Meridian Conference had standardized the *whole world* into time zones, with Greenwich Mean Time as the benchmark.

This was probably the greatest achievement in humankind's efforts to get a handle on time. At long last, each country (or large region) had a consistent time, and it was possible to know easily what time it was somewhere else, making it easier to travel, communicate, and do business. There is, however, one big drawback to this system: in most places, now, it is no longer the "natural" time. To tell the time, instead of looking at the sun, you look at your watch, and your watch is set according to a central authority. This certainly makes life more convenient, but it is not completely consistent with nature.

The belief in time as linear got another boost from the new theories and discoveries of the late nineteenth and early twentieth centuries.[6] The theory of evolution affirmed the idea of direction and progress. The Big Bang theory gave a scientific basis for the beginning of time. The expansion of democracy and civil rights confirmed our faith in the idea of progress.

Perhaps the most striking indication of the triumph of linear time has been the invention of digital clocks. Analogue clocks, with their big hand and little hand going round and round, give us a strong visual suggestion that time is cyclical. But with digital clocks, time really does look like it's adding up. Time is now displayed on your watch, on your phone, on your computer . . . *as a number.*

The belief that time is linear (and progressive) has now almost completely eclipsed the idea that time is cyclical. We no longer feel embedded in natural cycles, nor do we think of life as repeating itself. Industrialized countries think only of progress and growth. We believe that our lives should "add up" to something. We like to believe that we are getting somewhere.

Yet certain twentieth-century discoveries, and particularly Einstein's special theory of relativity, have cast doubt on the idea of linear time, and shown that time is neither absolute nor objective. Einstein's theory states that time, space, and motion are deeply related to one another. The time at which an event occurs actually depends on how far you are from that event, how fast you're moving, and in which direction. (This theory was later proven by an experiment in which an atomic clock, carried at high speed in an airplane, was shown to tick more slowly than an atomic clock on the ground.)

According to Einstein, there is no scientifically verifiable *now* that is true for everybody at once: everybody's time is different. There is *your* now and *my* now, but there is no objective *the* now. It's not the same time everywhere in the universe. Einstein proved that time is relative.

(Although Einstein's theory came as a shock, if we look closely, we can see some "evidence" for it in our everyday experience. When we speak of *time*, we often speak in terms of *space*: we say *length* of time and *amount* of time and *block* of time. We say that our days are *full* or *crowded*. We say that we *need some space* when we really *want some time*. We give our children a *time out*, but this also means some *space alone*.)

One of the most shocking conclusions from Einstein's discovery is that an event can be in the past for one observer but still in the future for another. Einstein actually concluded that "the past, present and future are only illusions, even if stubborn ones."[7] This is a serious challenge to the concept of linear time: without past, present, and future, how can we say that time moves forward? How can we think of time as a line? And if time isn't marching on, what is it?

With past and future relative, we can no longer think of time as laid out in a direction. Physicists now speak seriously about what was once science fiction: time travel, parallel universes, and multiple realities. More importantly, if the past and future are not absolute, and are not laid out in a direction, we must drop our assumption that the past causes the present or the present causes the future. We may even have to drop the notion that anything is actually caused by anything.

It's becoming clear that linear time isn't the whole story. Some historians now believe that another perspective, called "chaotic time," is supplanting the linear view. This may not be something you've heard of, but it's probably something you've felt. "Chaotic time" describes a world in which we no longer have faith in a linear narrative. We no longer believe that we're getting anywhere, and we lose confidence that the future will be better than the past. We recognize that time is experienced differently for different people in different places. We have trouble telling a coherent story about our lives or our culture. Past, present and future combine in a complex dance that is not easy to organize. "Progress," if it exists, might not even be such a good thing. This makes some people feel queasy; it makes other people want to dance.

But no matter what our view of time, it's important to remember that clocks have never ever really measured it. Time just isn't a thing "out there" to be measured. This is the most persistent illusion of time that we have. The way in which we divide the day—into hours, minutes, and seconds—is just a convention. (Indeed, the definition of a second was revised as recently as 1997.) You might just as well divide the day into twelve hours (which some cultures have done) or ten hours (a decimal system that the French proposed after the Revolution). In fact, for nearly 2500 years, most cultures used a system known as "temporal hours," in which there were always twelve hours of daylight no matter what the time of year. In order to achieve this, the length of an "hour" actually varied with the seasons.

The truth of the matter is that no one really knows what time is. Says physicist Paul Davies, in the introduction to

About Time, his second book summarizing the scientific theories of time: ". . . you may well be even more confused about time after reading this book than you were before. That's all right; I was more confused myself after writing it."[8]

Some physicists today go even one step further. Says Julian Barbour, in his provocative book, *The End of Time*, ". . . the important thing is to get away from the idea that time is something. Time does not exist. All that exists are things that change. What we call time is—in classical physics at least— simply a complex of rules that govern the change."[9] In other words, we experience things changing, and we need rules to make sense of that change, and we call those rules: time. Whether that set of rules exists, really, or is just an impression or construction of our minds, is still a mystery.

● ● ●

If we can accept that no one really knows what time is, that it may not exist, and that even if it does exist, it's relative, this might actually help us in our attempt to master the moment. For if you really want to master the moment, you must first give up the idea that time is an absolute "thing" out there, ticking away, or that linear time is the only game in town. You must understand that time is—at least to some extent—a projection of our minds. You must begin to believe that you can separate yourself from your assumptions about time, at least momentarily.

Linear time certainly has its uses, but perhaps chaotic time will help us get off its treadmill. Absolute time certainly is efficient, but perhaps relative time will release us from its tyranny. Perhaps we can stop being such victims of time. Perhaps our experience of time can become more flexible. Perhaps we can learn to play with time, knowing that it isn't as real as we think. For it is only really possible to seize the moment when time itself is up for grabs.

PART 4

Advanced Training

The One-Breath Cycle

In this first stage of advanced training, you will learn how to reduce the length of the Portable Minute gradually, bringing it closer and closer to a moment. The important word here is gradually. Here's how it works:

Start with the average breathcount you've been using for the Portable Minute, and reduce this by just one inhalation and one exhalation. For example, if your average breathcount is thirty, reduce it to twenty-eight. There's no need to take deeper or slower breaths, or attempt to continue for a full minute. In other words, your Portable Minute becomes a Portable Less-than-a-Minute. You are learning to enter a state of tranquility in less time. Think of this as "quickness training"—endurance training in reverse.

Continue to do the warm-up and cool-down, and keep your eyes closed, as you have been. As always, drop your attention into your breathing. In this exercise, you should experience the same sense of peace that you felt in the Basic Minute, just more quickly.

After doing this for a week, reduce your breathcount by one more inhalation and exhalation. Do that for a week, and then keep going: reduce your breathcount by two per week, one week at a time.

If you find that you are losing something—that you're not quite touching the same depth as you did in a full minute— then add back some breaths, or even go back to the Basic Minute, until you are really ready. Remember, quickness can't be rushed.

But if you're happy with your progress, then continue reducing your breathcount, week by week, until you are able to reach the wonderful quality of a Basic Minute in just one inhalation and one exhalation. This is the One-Breath Cycle. With just one cycle of inhalation and exhalation, you are experiencing the cleansing, refreshing benefits that once took you a whole minute.

The One-Breath Cycle is very short, but it is immensely valuable. You can do it instead of an Emergency Minute, a Surprise Minute, or a Bonus Minute. But never do it in haste. Don't forget to do a short ritual beforehand and a short ritual afterwards. And make sure that you have completely exhaled before opening your eyes, and then open them very slowly. In other words, even though it's short, it deserves your full attention.

> Please work your way down to a One-
> Breath Cycle, one week at a time, and be
> fully comfortable with the One-Breath
> Cycle before doing the next exercise.

Letting Go of the Handles

So far, you have used the warm-up and cool-down to help you carve some special time out of ordinary life—some time out of time—in which to find something extraordinary. With the warm-up you said, "Here comes something special," and with the cool-down you said, "That was really something else." But we can get too dependent on rituals, and in this chapter, you will learn to do without them.

Letting go of rituals can trigger some anxiety. Without the rituals, you might worry, there will be nothing to frame or circumscribe your experience of peacefulness. There will be no "before" and no "after." You might even start to wonder why you're not having this experience all the time. What is holding you back from entering a state of serenity whenever you want? What is stopping your whole life from being inherently peaceful? Well, that is precisely why we drop the ritual: to bring up these questions.

Dropping the ritual helps you realize that life is even better when it's not carved up into units. Dropping the ritual helps you find the extraordinary in the ordinary, and even better, to realize that ordinary life is itself, already, extraordinary. Dropping the ritual helps you realize that the only difference between the ordinary and the extraordinary is how you focus your attention, how you perceive things, and how you choose to experience time. Dropping the ritual means that you might be able to choose to be more peaceful, right now, without needing any special preparations or conditions. Can you handle that?

**Please try a One-Breath Cycle
now, without the rituals.**

If this change feels too sudden or intense, just drop one of the rituals at a time—either the warm-up or the cool-down. In times of stress, or when you're feeling unfocused, it's perfectly okay to reinstate a ritual. The key idea is to learn that you can choose, simply and without fanfare, to close your eyes and enter a state of deeper peace, right now, just by stopping what you're doing to be present in your breath. At any time of the day, with no special conditions, you can just be.

Without the rituals, the One-Breath Cycle becomes even more portable and useful. You can do it almost anywhere and almost any time: waiting at a traffic light, standing in line, sitting in a meeting. You can do it just before sending an email— to make sure that you're sure. You can do it after signing a contract, now that you're committed. In fact, the One-Breath Cycle can be a bookend for any important event, project, or even thought.

In this sense, the One-Breath Cycle actually becomes a ritual itself: you can use it as a warm-up or cool-down for anything. Simply withdraw your attention from the world, drop into your breathing, and tap into your natural peacefulness. No one even has to notice.

On those days when you are inundated by the demands of others, or just getting no time and no space to yourself, you now have an extraordinary resource that you can do almost anywhere, at a moment's notice. You have become a One-Breath Master. (You're still some distance from a moment, but you're getting close.)

Please try the One-Breath Cycle without the handles, at least once a day for seven days, before continuing. (Remember to exhale fully and to open your eyes very slowly.)

A Moment's Notice

By now, those days when you needed a whole minute and all those props—a timer, a warm-up, and solitude—just to find some peace, must seem like a distant memory, the Stone Age of your practice. Now your practice takes so little time, it hardly takes any time at all. It's hard to imagine that there is even further to go. It's hard to believe that there is yet another prop to take away. But there is.

Now that you can do the One-Breath Cycle whenever and wherever you want, it's time to let go of control a little. It's time to let the world decide when it's time for your One-Breath Cycle. Of course, this isn't the way we've been taught to live our lives. We want to be in control of our schedules. We want to be in control of time. But in this exercise, the idea is to let the world remind you to do a One-Breath Cycle at times of its choosing. This is actually an important component of mastery, for a master must be ready for action all the time, without any notice at all. This exercise is inspired by the famous "telephone meditation" taught by the Zen teacher Thich Nhat Hanh. He suggests that when the phone rings, instead of jumping up immediately from what you're doing to answer it, use the first ring as an occasion to pause and take a deep breath. Then answer the phone. But you don't have to use a telephone for this: you can use whatever trigger or cue you like. Each time you hear a church bell, do a One-Breath Cycle. Or each time there's a commercial break. Or each time you come to the end of a paragraph.

You can experiment with triggers that are more frequent and less frequent, or you can try having multiple triggers. You can try having a Trigger-of-the-Week or having different triggers for different places—home and work, town and country. You can use anything as a trigger—doorbells, sirens, flushing the toilet, the honking of a horn, the squawk of a seagull, the crying of a baby. The possibilities are endless. Consider doing this for the rest of your life.

> **Over the next day, notice and write down all the possible triggers for a One-Breath Cycle. Pick one trigger and use it for a week. Then pick a different trigger and use it for one week, before going further.**

Momentary Awareness

This next stage of training cannot actually be practiced, at least not in the same way as you've done so far. In this stage, instead of deciding to do your One-Breath Cycle at a particular time, or waiting for a predetermined trigger, simply let it happen spontaneously. Whenever it occurs to you, close your eyes and do a One-Breath Cycle, with full attention. Do it as soon as the thought comes to mind. Like now.

Do this with no cue whatsoever—just whenever and wherever it happens. Allow it to happen as often as it happens. Your training so far means that you no longer need any rituals or counting. Just close your eyes, be present in your breathing, and notice it fully. Then go back to what you're doing or thinking. Don't worry about how much time this will take. As you probably have realized, each time you do this you are not losing time, but finding it.

While I recommend that you keep practicing any and all of the exercises you have learned so far, by now you have probably noticed something remarkable. Without formal practice, and without any handles, you are having flashes of stillness throughout the day. For a second or two, many times throughout your day, you find yourself taking a deep breath and returning to the stillness that you now know intimately. In other words, you now realize that life is a series of triggers offering you countless opportunities to be peaceful. Instead of *you* seeking stillness, stillness is seeking you. Stillness begins to show itself as your true nature. You are ready to meet the moment.

PART 5

Meeting the Moment

What the Moment Is

In reducing the length of the Basic Minute bit by bit, you have indeed been getting closer to a moment. But what is a moment, really? As we've seen, time is not so easy to define; the moment is even less so. How could you possibly measure a moment? Could you find it on a map? Could you catch it in your hands? Is there a single timepiece that has ever clocked a moment?

I would like to offer this "thought exercise" to help you understand what a moment is (and why it is so hard to grasp). Imagine a line extending from deep in your past to far in your future. This is the line of time, the imaginary line on which you plot your life. Most of the time, your mind is occupied with an extended segment of this line: your thoughts or feelings about the past or the future. You are remembering, regretting, romanticizing, reconstructing. Or you are craving things that you don't yet have, working toward imagined outcomes, daydreaming about where you'd like to be someday.

Now imagine that you are reeling in that line, pulling it in toward you, from both directions at the same rate. As it converges on you, right where you are, at some point there will be no past and no future—no *length* of time left. This dimensionless point—with no extension in either direction—is right now. *This* is the moment.

The past and the future are like ghosts that haunt our minds and distract us from what is actually happening now. These ghosts are afraid of the moment, because they don't have any real existence in it: the past is just a memory (and not a terribly accurate one), and the future is just a fantasy. The reason why you can experience such peace in a moment, and only in a moment, is that you are not, in the moment, carrying the past or running after the future. In the moment, you stop chasing these phantoms, and they stop chasing you.

Because the moment doesn't exist for any *length* of time, it is not a *unit* of time. Indeed, the moment isn't a "thing" at all—which is why it can't be grasped. The moment, I believe, is actually an experience—the experience in which time gives way to timelessness. In other words, the moment is time's vanishing point. It is so small that it is actually huge, so infinitesimal that it is actually infinite.

When you are fully in the moment, your conventional experience of time is suspended, as if time itself stops. And this is why being in the moment is so extraordinary, and so desired by so many spiritual seekers: in the moment, you touch eternity.

And in the moment, this liberation from time, many other things can happen, spontaneously. You might realize something about yourself. You might have a new idea. You might experience the essential interconnection between you and all things. You might feel the urge to smile—for no reason at all. You might explode with laughter or tears at the perfection of it all. You might even experience the world from a much, much bigger perspective.

It's also possible, in the moment, that you won't experience anything. In other words, you simply cease to be: there is no you, so you aren't there to experience it. This can be the most momentous moment of all. Indeed, the moment is so extraordinary that there really aren't any words to describe it. The Zen monk Saigyo put it this way:

What it is
I know not;
But with the gratitude,
my tears fall.

Before the Moment

As you get closer to the moment, some strange things might start to happen. You might find that your body starts to shake. You might find yourself thinking "I'm not going *there.*" You might feel as if your head will explode. More likely your mind will experience all kinds of ideas and distractions— some of them quite clever—just to keep you from getting close to a moment. How strange: here you are, so close to something you have been working toward for months, or maybe years, and it seems as if you're running in the opposite direction. Why is that?

Being in the moment requires that we drop our conventional sense of self, but we don't really like doing that. Our "self" is built on memories of past experiences (and the lessons we've "learned" from them) and our hopes and expectations for the future, none of which exists in the moment. But we spend so much time "living" in the past and the future that we don't know who we'd be without them.

At an even more fundamental level, our sense of self is based on the *idea* that there *is* a past and future. The very idea of "identity" is based on the assumption that something about us continues over time—that we exist as essentially the same person from moment to moment. So when you drop the idea of past and future, you also drop the concept of "you." This makes the experience of the moment, in its deepest form, truly humbling.

The experience of the moment is actually a death—not a death of your body, but of who you *think* you are. This is why it can be scary: because you don't know who you'd be without you. But what is dying is just your *idea* of yourself— what mystics call the "small self." And when this small self dies, something greater appears. When you get out of the way of yourself, what appears is both magnificent and subtle. We will explore some of the more dramatic variations of this experience in the next chapter. But to put it simply, when you let go of your assumptions and expectations, you become open to being surprised. You allow life (or God) to show you something else.

The nice thing about the One-Moment Method is that this "death" happens a little bit at a time, so it's less of a shock. Indeed, it has probably already happened—momentarily of course—during each of your Basic Minutes and even your One-Breath Cycles. Somewhere in each of those experiences, there was probably a moment in which you were so present in your breath that there was no "you." You were no longer aware of yourself. (You may not have noticed it, of course, because you weren't there.) As I said previously: when you are truly in the moment, you don't just stop *doing*, you stop *youing*. And that's why it's so refreshing—for the ultimate stress in life is our attempt to maintain an idea of ourselves from one moment to the next.

Some Famous Moments

Some moments are so momentous that whether you are prepared for them or not, you notice them. These moments are like flashes of light, so brilliant in the truth that they reveal, and such a dramatic reversal of what we expect, that they change the course of our lives, and sometimes the lives of many others. Sometimes they are called miracles. They have also been called "peak experiences," because they suggest the highest part of our nature. In this chapter, we'll look at some of the most remarkable peaks.

Eureka!

One day in Ancient Greece, while lowering his body into the bathtub, the mathematician Archimedes suddenly realized an important principle about the displacement of water. He was so excited by this discovery, the story goes, that he leapt out of the bath and ran through the streets, naked, shouting "Eureka!" ("I've found it!"). In his exuberance, Archimedes bequeathed to us an enduring image of the joy of sudden discovery.

The birth of a creative idea—even if you've spent years preparing for it—happens when you least expect it. Artists and writers tend to be on the lookout for moments like these, constantly, which is why they usually keep a notebook handy. J.K. Rowling had quite a moment like this on the train one day, when all the characters and details of Harry Potter, she says, "just fell into my head." She had the good sense to trust this moment: fifteen years later, her sixth Harry Potter book sold 6.9 million copies in the United States in just one day. Isn't it possible that a creative idea is hovering in the universe, quite near you, right now, just waiting to be noticed?

Hitting Bottom

Sometimes it seems that no matter how determined we are to stay upbeat, life keeps bringing us down. This is most noticeable, and most extreme, when people are struggling with addiction. They may keep trying to get high or stay high until they actually collapse, losing everything: home, family, job, money, and health. "Hitting bottom" describes this moment of absolute collapse. But, for those who survive it, the results can be extraordinary, for the moment of hitting *bottom* is often followed by a moment of hitting *top*.

Bill W., founder of Alcoholics Anonymous, describes how, after a relapse of severe drinking, he lay in the hospital, in the "blackest depression" of his life, and began to note every wrong he had committed against others. Accepting that he was powerless over alcohol, he began to pray. He says:

The result was instant, electric, beyond description. The place seemed to light up, blinding white. I knew only ecstasy and seemed on a mountain. A great wind blew, enveloping and penetrating me. To me, it was not of air, but of Spirit. Blazing, there came the tremendous thought. "You are a free man." Then the ecstasy subsided. I now found myself in a new world of consciousness which was suffused by a Presence. One with the universe, a great peace stole over me.[10]

This moment was Bill's turnaround. His experience of hitting bottom led not just to his own recovery, but eventually to the formation of more than 100,000 Alcoholics Anonymous groups, and many similar groups that help people with other kinds of addiction. It seems that those people who survive hitting bottom find a vitality that they never had before. In a moment, they face the worst thing imaginable, and having faced it, are transformed.

Shining Moments and Defining Moments

There are moments in life when our true potential shines forth from our otherwise ordinary personality. These shining and defining moments often end up quoted in tributes: wedding speeches, eulogies, or—if we're running for political office—television commercials. Although these moments often happen by surprise, when life just forces the best out of us, some people actually seek them, taking on incredibly challenging, even dangerous, tasks, just to find out "what they're made of."

Of course, not all defining moments are shining: we are also defined by failure, vulnerability and foolishness. Perhaps the best tributes capture the extremes of personality—the highs and the lows, the wisdom and the folly: those moments that convey our true personality, with all its contradictions.

Breakthrough

After a period of struggle or stagnation, a new reality can emerge quite unexpectedly. Perhaps you have been trying to learn to ice skate, with no sense of progress, feeling very frustrated as you clomp clomp across the ice, and then all of a sudden, you're gliding. Or perhaps, at work, your team has been having a protracted argument, and then someone laughs, and then everyone laughs, and there is suddenly a new shared understanding.

One of the surest signs that there's a breakthrough nearby is when you (or your group) are in a state of high agitation: it feels as if you are going to explode. This moment can be quite precarious, however, because when you're close to breakthrough, you are also close to breakdown. Having supported many individuals and groups through this moment, I have come to believe that one of the keys to achieving a breakthrough is the ability to stay present with the enormous tension of the crisis. Instead of trying to stop what is happening, or control what is happening, or run back to an earlier situation that felt more stable, you have to stay with the tension until you see the new idea that is trying to emerge.

Often the first appearance of a breakthrough comes from an unexpected angle and is very small, and thus very easy to miss. Like a tiny, rare seedling, sprouting in your lawn, it is so easily mowed down. In these situations, it often takes an outsider—a therapist, consultant, or good friend—to notice the new idea and put a small fence around it. This keeps it safe, helps you notice it, and holds some space for its growth.

The more we are able to be aware of the moment and be prepared for the moment, the more we can do this for ourselves and others. We can be ready for everything to change. Learning how to let go of a habitual position—to refresh our perspective continually—is one of the best ways to ensure that life is just one breakthrough after another.

The Moment of No Return

A moment of no return occurs when you realize that a decision is truly irreversible. In that moment, you accept the new world as it is. You stop pulling against the way things are, accept the present reality, and live from that moment forward.

The story of human history is built on political, cultural, and military moments of no return. You have probably experienced some very dramatic ones in your personal and professional life. But really, every single moment is a moment of no return. Life is always how it is—never how it might have been, and there is no going back. Even if you could go back to an earlier situation, you would go back with the awareness you have now, and so it would be different. Heraclitus put it this way: you can't step in the same river twice.

The Moment of Truth

Life would be so much simpler if everyone told the truth. Yet because not everybody tells the truth, and nobody tells the truth all the time, we seem to need moments in which it becomes impossible *not* to tell the truth. In a moment of truth, we may want to squirm and wriggle, but it feels as if we are pinned to the spot. *Gotcha!*

The odd thing is that, when you are forced to admit something that you've done—told a lie, taken a bribe, fixed a race, had an affair, eaten the cookies—if you really admit it, and take responsibility for it, it can turn out to be the best thing that ever happened to you. To "atone" for our sins literally means to be "at one with" them or—as we say now—to "own" them or "own up" to them.

Of course, not all moments of truth involve admitting fault. Sometimes a moment of truth just involves realizing the truth about how you feel, telling the truth about who you are, or speaking the truth about what's happening around you. This can be an enormous liberation. One of the great figures in the history of American civil rights, Rosa Parks, made a simple, defiant action one day when she refused to yield her seat on a bus to a white man. Said Parks of this moment, "When the white driver stepped back toward us, when he waved his hand

and ordered us up and out of our seats, I felt a determination cover my body like a quilt on a winter night. . . . I felt a light suddenly shine through the darkness."[11] This was her moment of truth. It led to a moment of no return.

Rebirth

Although we have each been born once, it seems that many of us feel a need to repeat the experience. Indeed, the symbolism of rebirth can be found cross-culturally—in religious literature, fairy tales, mythology, and even in modern political speeches and news reports. It seems that, whenever we face a major transition, we draw on the symbolism of rebirth.

The psychiatrist Stanislav Grof has identified four typical stages of the rebirth process, echoing actual childbirth: we begin in a state of innocence (the womb), experience a crisis (the onset of labor), struggle through a difficult and dangerous transition (the birth canal), and then suddenly find ourselves in a new world (birth), a world that we couldn't possibly have anticipated. Emerging into the light, we feel released from old patterns of behavior, and released from the enormous tension we felt just a moment before.

The moment of rebirth is directly preceded by an experience of psychological death, when our old patterns of behavior reach an unbearable climax. This is a moment of enormous challenge, but also of extraordinary opportunity, for if we can realize the inner psychological change demanded of us, then in just a moment, everything can change. Profound release is possible no matter how dark or stuck life seems. Indeed, Grof's work suggests that at the moment when our suffering is most acute, we are actually closest to liberation.

Transfiguration

Of all possible moments, the most extraordinary must surely be the moment of transfiguration. In the Biblical account, Jesus leads Peter, James and John up a mountain to pray. Then:

> . . . his clothes became shining, exceedingly white, like snow, such as no launderer on earth can whiten them. And Elijah appeared to them with Moses, and they were talking with Jesus.

Peter, James and John had been "heavy with sleep" but on seeing this, became "fully awake."

> And a cloud came and overshadowed them; and a voice came out of the cloud, saying: "This is My beloved Son, hear Him!" Suddenly, when they had looked around, they saw no one anymore, but only Jesus with themselves.   (Mark 9: 2–8)

The Hindu story of transfiguration is told in *The Song of God*, one of the most revered Hindu texts. In this story, Krishna reveals his true nature as the god Vishnu to his disciple, Arjuna. This happens, for Arjuna, in a moment of profound release after a period of great suffering. Granted a blinding vision of Krishna's "imperishable" form, he says:

> I see you beginningless, endless. . .
> lighting the whole universe with splendor.

> Again and again I bow to you,
> from all sides, in every direction.
> Majesty infinite in power,
> You pervade—no, you are—all things.[12]

It's very unlikely that you or I will experience a moment quite like this. But the reaction of Peter, James, John and Arjuna suggests how we might feel in such a moment: humbled, amazed, transfixed, and wide awake.

Enlightenment

The moment of enlightenment contains some of the dazzling characteristics of transfiguration, but the difference is that anyone can do it. The most famous person who did it (and made it very popular) was Siddhartha Gautama. After searching for years to understand the cause of suffering, Siddhartha simply sat down and concentrated on his breathing, vowing not to move until he had realized the truth. He sat through many temptations and distractions until finally coming to see that the root of suffering is in craving. When his craving stopped, he saw reality unobstructed, with a clear mind, and became known as the Buddha: someone who is awake.

The most dramatic examples of enlightenment are sudden, ecstatic, and overwhelming. But enlightenment can also be experienced gradually, like the rising of the sun. Although Buddhist teachers urge students to work hard to achieve this experience of enlightenment, they also acknowledge that it is in our trying so hard that we distance ourselves from it, for the more we want it, the more we keep ourselves in a state of wanting. Enlightenment is not a distant goal: it is always present.

Grace

The origin of the word *grace* and the word *gift* are closely related. Both come from the Greek *charis*. Indeed, the moment of grace comes to us as a gift, which means we can't really look for it. But its existence reminds us that anything, truly anything, can happen in a moment. Theologian Paul Tillich reminds us that, even when our lives seem to be on a downward spiral, or everything is hopeless, or we have done something truly terrible, and logic tells us that all is lost, something else might happen:

> We cannot transform our lives, unless we allow them to be transformed by that stroke of grace. It happens; or it does not happen. And certainly it does not happen if we try to force it upon ourselves, just as it shall not happen so long as we think, in our self-complacency, that we have no need of it. Grace strikes us when we are in great pain and restlessness. It strikes us when we walk through

the dark valley of a meaningless and empty life. It strikes us when we feel that our separation is deeper than usual, because we have violated another life, a life which we loved, or from which we were estranged. It strikes us when our disgust for our own being, our indifference, our weakness, our hostility, and our lack of direction and composure have become intolerable to us. It strikes us when, year after year, the longed-for perfection of life does not appear, when the old compulsions reign within us as they have for decades, when despair destroys all joy and courage. Sometimes at that moment a wave of light breaks into our darkness, and it is as though a voice were saying: "You are accepted. You are accepted, accepted by that which is greater than you, and the name of which you do not know. Do not ask for the name now; perhaps you will find it later. Do not try to do anything now; perhaps later you will do much. Do not seek for anything; do not perform anything; do not intend anything. Simply accept the fact that you are accepted!" If that happens to us, we experience grace. After such an experience we may not be better than before, and we may not believe more than before. But everything is transformed. . . And in the light of this grace we perceive the power of grace in our relation to ourselves. We experience moments in which we accept ourselves, because we feel that we have been accepted by that which is greater than we. If only more such moments were given to us!¹³

●   ●   ●

In this chapter, I have described a few of the most famous kinds of moments, the moments of most dramatic turnaround. Sometimes these moments, as Tillich suggests, come at the absolute depth of a crisis. Sometimes, as with Archimedes, they just happen when you're getting into the bath. In other words, we can't predict when life will change, or when we will suddenly see things more clearly. But we can certainly try to be ready.

After the Moment

If you ever do experience a dramatic moment like those in the last chapter, you might feel very pleased with yourself. You might want to start telling people about it. You might want to jump up and down and yell "I'm free!" You might even want to write a book, like this one, telling people how they can do it, too.

You might also realize that, when doing any of those things, you aren't experiencing the moment any more. For as soon as you think about *that* moment, tell people about *that* moment, or even remember *that* moment or want it again, you have separated yourself from *this* moment. You may even start to feel a bit down in the dumps, back to business, fallen to the ground. Then, whenever you come up against an obstacle, instead of dealing with it as the moment that is here now, you'll want to run back to a moment you had months or years ago. You might even be tempted to begin a very long process of searching to find "it" again.

But being in the moment means a radical acceptance of what is happening now. You don't have to like or agree with what's happening now. The world is not always a nice place.

But any true experience of the moment begins with facing the truth of what is happening now, whether you like it or not.

After an experience of the moment, no matter how momentous, the best thing to do is another One-Breath Cycle, or just see what happens in *this* moment. You may not experience anything mind-blowing. This moment may pale in comparison to that moment. You may not even experience anything. But at least you're putting yourself in position. In other words, it's more important to be in the habit of returning to your breath, and to be committed to this practice, than it is to experience something dramatic.

The ultimate proof of the One-Moment Method is not whether you achieve eternal bliss, or have an astonishing experience, but whether you approach each moment with an acceptance for it being what it is. In other words, the proof is the practice. Each moment is what it is. In another moment, it will be different. And that will be what it is, too. As soon as we stop trying to make what *is* into something that it *isn't*, or wishing it were something else, we relax. And everything begins. Again.

What the Moment Isn't

There's a lot of talk these days about "being in the moment" and "living for the moment." But some of these ideas can be downright dangerous, and I don't want you to think that this book endorses them.

The popular idea of "being in the moment" can be used to justify selfishness and hedonism. "No matter what is happening," it suggests, "let's party." I have seen many people use this mixed-up mantra to disengage with their true feelings, the reality of life around them, or the consequences of their actions. Clearly human beings in the "developed" world have been "living for the present" so much that we are endangering our own survival.

If "being in the moment" means just being in the *nice* moments or the *fun* moments, then we are seriously cutting reality in half. Being in the moment often involves facing some truth about ourselves or the world. In the true experience of the moment, there can actually be a profound reckoning. This might mean simply acknowledging that right now we are feeling helpless or hopeless, angry or afraid, and for just a moment, we stop trying to figure out how to stop feeling that way. We just experience it.

Of course, in the moment, you might realize that you are very happy. You might even experience great bliss. There's nothing wrong with that. But if feeling happy depends on avoiding bad news, or what's happening in the world, or people who "get you down," then it's not a very secure happiness. And if you then go into the next moment holding on to that feeling of happiness, afraid of losing it, and refusing to notice what is happening in the new moment, then you are no longer in *this* moment: you are clinging to *that* moment.

When people suggest "living for the moment," they are probably trying to avoid an experience of their own suffering or the suffering of other people. The consequence of this can be severe: it can keep them from experiencing real content-ment. Real contentment comes not from picking out the "good" or "positive" experiences, or even the "high" experi-ences or "peak" experiences, but from being *able* to be present with whatever is happening now. In this way, life becomes not a constant party, but a constant opportunity to deepen our well-being . . . and the well-being of others.

Being in the moment can be hard sometimes. Sometimes you will want to be anywhere *but* in the moment, to experi-ence anything but what is happening now. There are terrible things that may happen to you. There will be failures and ill-nesses and setbacks. There will be many days that you just feel lousy. But when life is overwhelming, do what you always do, what you have learned to do: a One-Breath Cycle. And then, when you're ready, do another. Sometimes, it's the only thing you can count on.

PART 6
Very Advanced Training

In your experience of the Basic Minute, Portable Minute, and the One-Breath Cycle, you have been taking some time out of time—some time for *just being*. In other words, you have learned how to drop out of time. But if practiced to excess, this could become a problem. You might start to resent your life, or even resent time itself. You might want to spend all your time out of time—doing the Basic Minute, as it were, forever. But as that would be an incomplete understanding of stillness, this part of the book aims to complete the picture.

This next set of exercises will involve a slight shift of focus. You still begin each exercise with your attention settled in your breathing, as you've learned. But the next step involves expanding your awareness to include something in the world "outside" you as well. Staying anchored in your breathing (so you don't drift away), you find a middle place, an experience that is part you and part the world.

In this way, you learn to experience not just the peace of being, but the peace of being *in* time. Eventually you will find that stillness is not time *out* of life, but *is* your life, and takes no time at all.

Looking Around

With the One-Breath Cycle, you learned how to experience stillness with just one inhalation and exhalation, more or less at will. But you're still doing this with your eyes closed, and most of the rest of your life is lived with your eyes open. The One-Breath Cycle, as you've practiced it, is a profound *inner* experience, but life goes on *out there*. So the next step is to try to do the One-Breath Cycle while seeing the world.

At first, this may seem like a shock. If you have been practicing the One-Breath Cycle, experiencing some time each day out of time, you may have come to see the world "out there" as a distraction from the peace of just being "in here." With this new exercise, the idea is to experience the peace of just being *while also* seeing the dazzling, distracting, dance of life—the array of time.

This is not as hard as you might suspect. In fact, it's quite soft. As my friend Troup Matthews used to say, "Don't try harder, try softer." To do this, you must open your heart to embrace the universe. You must welcome what you see in front of you, whatever it is, for it is not the enemy of your peacefulness, but part of it.

Do this slowly at first. Start by looking at something beautiful and pleasing—something that is easy for you to enjoy. This could be a flower, a view from the window, a piece of jewelry, or a photo of someone you love. Do a One-Breath Cycle with your eyes open, looking at this pleasing thing. Notice the effect it has on you. Allow yourself to feel, fully, what you're feeling. This feeling is the dynamic interplay between you and something else, something that seems to be "outside" of you or separate from you. Imagine breathing this feeling into your body, bringing it all the way into your heart.

> **Please pause to try this now. Just find
> the most pleasing thing to look at that's
> already right near you, where you are, and
> do a One-Breath Cycle while looking at
> it. Notice the effect on how you feel.**

As you advance in this practice, try doing it in more challenging situations—when what you see in front of you seems ugly, trivial, depressing, or just difficult to like. For example, the next time you see a television news report showing scenes of poverty, crime, environmental damage, or war, don't change the channel or freeze in horror. Simply see what's there, feel what you feel, and breathe in and out.

This exercise can bring up some powerful resistance: "Why should I pay attention to something depressing?" But remember that being at peace is not really being at peace if it is dependent on everything being just the way you like it.

Being peaceful means being *inherently* peaceful, no matter what is happening. This doesn't mean you have to like what's happening or agree with it, but you can learn to be at peace in the midst of it, while still experiencing it. If you try to live in a protected bubble, you are always living in a precarious way: the bubble could burst. Genuine peacefulness has nothing to fear from the truth of life. *If it's true, it's for you.*

So see if you can be with everything that you see. See if you can widen your attention to embrace the whole world. You may some day find that you and the world are not so different after all.

Do a One-Breath Cycle the next time you see something shocking or depressing. In fact, any time you see something that you don't want to see, try doing a One-Breath Cycle. Please practice this for one month before trying the next exercise.

Moving Around

Now you are ready for the next step. Literally. Instead of being still while sitting still, now you learn to be still while on the move. Please take it slowly.

Normally, when you're on the go, you're not conscious of what you're doing. You are just focused on where you're going—until you bump into someone, stumble down a step, or slip on the ice . . . and wake up. But if you're only focused on the goal, you miss out on the process. You are living in an idea of a future moment, not in what's happening in *this* moment. And one thing you can be sure of: as soon as you get where you're going, your mind will create a new journey, a new problem to solve, a new goal. So in not experiencing the journey, you are not experiencing your life.

The exercise in this chapter helps you to be present right where you are. If you practice this exercise slowly, in this very simple way, the benefits will reverberate throughout your life. You may think, "It's just walking." But even walking can be quite subtle: each step contains many steps, so it's worth paying attention to them.

There are two levels to this exercise. Here is the first:

Level One:

1. Stand still.
2. Look gently at the ground (or the floor) in front of you.
3. Feel the contact between your feet and the ground (or the floor).
4. Do a One-Breath Cycle.

This exercise is immensely useful when you're out and about. So many of us walk around with no awareness of where our feet are placed, whether we are physically balanced, or even where we are. (This is surely a major cause of accidents.) I use this exercise to punctuate a journey—for example, when I turn a corner, reach the top of a hill, or just before I ring the doorbell. I use it especially when everybody is rushing around me—in train stations or on city sidewalks at rush hour. It's also a good exercise to do before lifting something heavy. Just get in the habit of stopping for a moment, right where you are, feeling your feet on the ground, and breathing. You will be amazed at how much stress this dissolves. Although it may slow you down a bit, it will also prevent some major missteps.

Please pause to try Level One now.

The next step in this exercise is much more complicated and involves some coordination. It requires maintaining all the awareness of Level One while also taking a step—which is no small feat. Here's how to do it:

Level Two:

1. Stand still.

2. Look gently at the ground (or the floor) in front of you.

3. Feel the contact between your feet and the ground (or the floor).

4. Shift all your weight to the right foot.

5. Breathe in while lifting the left foot.

6. Put the left foot down just in front of you, shifting about half your weight to it, and exhaling fully.

7. Stop.

When you first try this, you may feel a bit uncoordinated, but in time you'll find that it feels quite natural. If you have some extra time, try doing it with the other foot: one foot after the other, one step at a time. Maybe some day you can even try doing it all the way across the room, out the door, down the driveway, or across town. But wherever this exercise takes you, try to experience each step as if it were your only destination.

Please pause to try Level Two now.

Being Around

I have heard many spiritual teachers say that we spend far too much time *doing*. They remind us that we are human *beings*, not human *doings*. Well, with the exercises in this book, you have probably become quite good at *just being*. For some spiritual traditions, it stops right there.

This is because so much of our spiritual inheritance has been passed down to us by monks or nuns who lived cloistered in monasteries, or hermits who abandoned society altogether. These pioneers certainly achieved great wisdom, but often this was at the expense of participation in the ordinary world, and sometimes even in denial or hatred of this world. Their teachings, and the example of their lives, have given us a dangerous belief that serenity is only possible apart from the world or in another world or in the next world. This leaves us very little hope, and very few techniques, for finding serenity in this world. We believe that serenity can only be found where there's not much to do: in church, in a monastery, on retreat, in the wilderness, or in the next life. Not only is this discouraging, it lets us off the hook. We believe that spiritual awareness—or a strong commitment to spiritual practice—is for them, not us.

So let's not forget about, or dismiss, the importance of doing. Life is made of rest *and* activity, stasis *and* growth, being *and* doing. Pure stillness can't be the goal; activity can't be the problem. Remember that even when you're sitting still, and even when you're sleeping, there's tremendous activity in your body: lungs expanding and contracting, heart pumping, neurons firing—to name just some of the constant goings-on.

The ultimate challenge is to find the peace of being *in the midst of* doing, to practice being *while* doing this and that. The Tibetans have a nice phrase for this, a phrase they consider so important that they repeat it all the time: *Om mani padme hum.* This is translated as "the jewel of eternity is found in the lotus of birth and death." The "jewel of eternity" is another way of saying pure being, and "the lotus of birth and death" is another way of saying the world of time, or in other words, doing. So this phrase means that in spite of any fantasies of escape we might have, the ultimate experience of *being* is found in the midst of *doing.* Ultimately, being "in the moment" does not mean just experiencing timelessness, but experiencing *timelessness in time*—in other words, stillness while on the go.

Up until now, you have turned your attention away from what you were doing to be in your breathing. But now the challenge is to notice your breathing while doing what you're doing. Say, for example, that you have learned to pause, when grinding coffee or washing the car, for a One-Breath Cycle. Now, you don't stop grinding or washing. Now you breathe *into* and *with* what you're doing. You notice your breathing *while* doing what you're doing. You do both at once. You *be* both at once. In this breathing-and-doing there is no you and there is no what-you're-doing: you simply are what you're doing.

**Please take a moment to try this
now, whatever you're doing.**

This practice can be very energizing, but also very challenging. It may sometimes feel like a big stretch, as if you have one foot on one shore and the other foot on the other shore and you're hanging somewhere in the middle: it's that difficult. It may help to put some extra enthusiasm into what you're doing—even if it is a rather ordinary task.

Whenever you need to, you can return to a One-Breath Cycle or even a Basic Minute. These can still provide a refuge for you, a place to which you return for rejuvenation. But just remember that there is no retreat from life. The way to find peace is not to run to moments of *just being* in order to have energy for the difficult job of *doing*, but to accept that life is made of doing whatever it is that needs to be done.

By focusing on *being and doing*, you will find that doing is itself a way of being. In fact, it is the nature of your being. And as you practice this, you will feel more in touch with the continuous flow of being and doing—what could be called "peaceful doing."

Mastery begins when you no longer need to carve out a moment from time in order to pay attention to your breathing, to practice being, or to experience peace, but when you experience the peace of being in the crazy chaos of doing.

Now, all throughout the day, you find yourself doing and breathing, doing and breathing, doing and breathing. You find yourself noticing that you're being, noticing that you're doing, noticing that you're noticing, even noticing that you're noticing, and all the while, breathing.

So see if you can be with everything. See if you can throw your being fully into everything you're doing. See if you can do what you're doing with that peaceful quality of being. Allow what you're doing to occupy your whole mind, with nothing in the way: no fantasies about the future, no memories of the past, no rushing, and no slowing down. This is still doing.

Eventually you may find that you and what-you're-doing are not really so different. It might even seem that you and the world are breathing as one. In moments like these, you might notice that everything gets a bit brighter, or comes into focus, as if the cacophonic sounds of an orchestra tuning up suddenly become harmonious. In moments like these, you are fully present in what you are doing and also know that you are not doing it. Something greater than you is doing what you're doing. You are almost done. And just beginning.

PART 7

The Miracle of
the Moment

Rest and Recreation

In this part of the book, you will learn some flexible, playful, and adaptable applications of the exercises you've learned so far. These exercises will help you to integrate your practice with everything that you do and to appreciate each moment as miraculous.

First, I must explain the concept of *continuous creation*. Actually, continuous creation is not a concept as much as an experience—the direct perception that there is no causal connection from one moment to the next. In other words, the entire universe is blinking into existence—whole—moment by moment.

A good way to understand continuous creation is through the metaphor of a movie. A movie is composed of still images, shown one at a time, very quickly. (The word "movie" comes from the phrase "moving picture.") Movies are like sophisticated versions of flipbooks—those small books made up of many pictures arranged in sequence—each one with a subtle difference. When you flip through a flipbook quickly, it seems that the figures in the pictures are moving, one causing the next. But the connection between the images is not *in* the images. The connection between the pictures is in your mind (and in the mind of whoever created the book). With movies, this technique is so sophisticated—twenty-four frames go by each second—that you don't even realize that the images are separate.

Continuous creation suggests that reality is created anew in each moment, and also that each moment is distinct. This is not the same thing as creationism, for it does not imply that the universe was created at some point in the past. And it's not in conflict with science. It is simply a way of seeing reality that has been experienced by spiritual masters in both theistic and non-theistic religions. It is the foundation of Hindu mysticism and it was expounded by twelfth-century Islamic scholar Abu Hamid Al-Ghazali. Zen scholar D.T. Suzuki put it this way: "My solemn proclamation is that a new universe is created every moment." The Christian mystic, Meister Eckhart, expressed it this way: "God is creating the entire universe, fully and totally, in this present now." Says Rabbi David Cooper:

> [In the Jewish mystical tradition] . . . the Now rests upon the palm of God's hand, so to speak. The dimension of this moment is supported in its entirety by the nature of the Divine. Thus there is a vital relationship between God and every aspect of creation. Each breath I draw is initiated, sustained, and nourished by the power of creation. Each event is permeated by the magic of the Divine Presence.[14]

To say that each moment is newly created also means that there is no inherent continuity from one moment to the next.

We can't be sure that what we do in this moment really is the cause of what happens in the next moment. We can't even be sure that the next moment will be. This way of thinking is not, of course, a typical way of looking at life: normally, we take continuity for granted. But continuity from one moment to the next, according to continuous creation, is an illusion.

The implications of continuous creation are that every moment is utterly brand new, unhindered by the past. In every moment, the world is being re-created. In the next moment, everything could be *completely* different. This opens up some fairly radical possibilities, which we'll explore in the next few chapters.

At the very least, the idea of continuous creation should make us think a little differently about "rest and recreation." Normally, when we want recreation, we fantasize about leisure activities, such as playing a sport or taking a cruise. But this kind of recreation just gives us a rest, which just enables us to come right back to our lives and accumulate more stress. Continuous creation suggests that if you want real rejuvenation, you don't want recreation but re-creation. You must experience yourself re-created, moment by moment. Fortunately, re-creation is what the One-Moment Method is all about.

The Moment of Choice

Consider the moment you wake up in the morning—the *very first moment* you wake up in the morning. In that moment, you are open and innocent—a blank slate—as if, during the night, you had completely forgotten yourself and returned to a place of pure possibility. Then, in the next moment, you remember. It all comes flooding in. You remember all your hopes and fears, stresses and strains, and you remember the day ahead of you. In other words, your innocent soul puts on a body worn down by time and experience, and that feeling of pure possibility is gone. So you face the day, not with an open mind, but with a host of expectations based on your past experience, even though *you can't possibly know what will happen.*

But what if you could stop yourself from putting on that creaky old set of expectations? What if you could live from that attitude of innocence—an attitude of "no attitude"—all throughout the day? When Christ said, "You must be as a child to enter the Kingdom of Heaven," I believe that he was referring to this essential openness that we each have, this feeling we have when just-waking-up. Surely this is also what Buddha meant when he spoke of our "original nature."

Isn't it wonderful that this openness is given to you, if only for a moment, each morning? I don't know why we are in such a rush to abandon it each day, and put on our assumptions, but perhaps we can learn not to. A good way to start, I believe, is simply to notice the first time we do it each morning.

So try this exercise: Do a One-Breath Cycle, lying down, the very moment you wake up. If you miss that moment, just do a One-Breath Cycle before you get out of bed. (If you tend to wake up quickly and then immediately start rushing, put a reminder by your bed the night before.) When you're accomplished at this, try doing a One-Breath Cycle sooner, even before you open your eyes. Then gradually, over time, try bringing the One-Breath Cycle closer to the actual moment of waking up.

Once you've done this for a while, try it in reverse. At some point later in the day, see if you can *take off your attitude*. See if you can return to the attitude of innocence you had on waking up. See if you can take off your assumptions as if they were a mask. See if you can unhook yourself. See if you can let yourself off the hook.

The point is that, in each moment, you have a radical choice about who and how you are. You can choose to not act as you have always done. You can choose whether to greet the next moment with a closed mind or open mind. If you can notice the moment *just before* your habits and expectations come rushing in, before they take over and crowd out your innocence, then you can take a breath and give yourself time to make a new choice. Gradually, over time, you will find that your original openness returns to refresh you, spontaneously, many times throughout the day, and there's no choice necessary.

Eternal Youth

Centuries ago, explorers searched for the "fountain of youth" and hoped that by drinking its waters, they could avoid old age and death. Nowadays, being far more sophisticated, we seek the fountain of youth in a pill from the doctor or a smoothie from the juice bar. Sure, medical science can prolong life as never before, but some of the effort we spend looking for eternal youth might be better spent looking for eternal youthfulness.

Youthfulness is not a quality you can find by aping the dress, musical tastes, or slang of teenagers. Youthfulness is *not* a willingness to go bungee jumping at age sixty-five. At its core, youthfulness is simply a quality of mind, a mindset that greets each moment with a sense of possibility. The One-Breath Cycle, I believe, is the fountain of youthfulness.

The reason for this, of course, is that youthfulness has all to do with having an open and curious mind. Imagine how the world looks to an infant: a continual source of amazement and a constant opportunity for experimentation and learning. Infants are born, naturally, with the spirit of creative artists and experimental scientists. (They lack some technical skills, of course.) By the time we are middle aged, however, we are so

sure we know how things work that we lose this sense of engaged curiosity with the world around us. We think we've seen
it all, done it all, and know it all. But we don't really know how
things work, and we have barely tapped the potential of our
creativity and ingenuity.

Although it's doubtful that we can ever capture again the
extraordinary sense of wonder of a child seeing the world
for the first time, there is no need for us to become bored or
believe that life is predictable. There is no need to lose our
sense of amazement at the extraordinary display that the world
puts on each day. The masters know that, as we age, we can
actually appreciate life more: we become more aware that
the simple fact of existence is a miracle. In other words, for a
master, youthfulness improves with time.

Advanced Time Management

In every moment, the "will to life" and the "threat of death" are fully present. For something to begin, something else must end. When something ends, something else begins. There's no way around it: everything new depends on the death of something old.

I don't mean this in a literal one-to-one kind of way. I don't mean that for each new baby born, someone has to die. What I mean is that each new state of being marks the end of another state of being. For example, on your first day of school, your life as a pre-schooler is over. When two corporations merge, their identities as independent organizations cease. When you get married, you are no longer single, and even if you get divorced someday, you will never again be a person who was never married.

In a deeper sense, in each moment, who you *were* is dying and who you *are becoming* is being born. I mean this psychologically, of course, but it's true physically as well: in every moment, some cells are being born and some cells are dying. You are changing, all the time. Birth is not something that just happened at the beginning of your life, and death is not just something that will happen at the end. Birth and death are happening right now. They are the components of existence. Every moment has an ending and a beginning. Every moment *is* an ending and a beginning.

So as you approach mastery of the moment, you may experience moments of great joy, when you perceive everything around you as radiant and new, and moments of great sadness, when you really understand that everything, yes everything, dies. To fully embrace the moment, you must embrace both of these perspectives as fundamental to being. You must allow these two extremely opposed forces to find some balance in your heart. Only when you realize this fully—accepting the movement of these two forces deep within you—can you truly be at peace.

Here are two practices that will help you to experience the birth and death of each moment—one focuses on ending and the other focuses on beginning.

Ending

Many people, as they approach death, begin to shed some of their conventional personality. Taking stock of their lives, they feel a need to finish their unfinished emotional business. They try to express all those feelings that they weren't able to express before, for they want to die in peace, having told the truth. Often they want to reconcile with estranged friends and family members, or to express love, forgiveness, regret, or gratitude.

But there's no need to wait until you are almost dead for this. Just imagine you are about to die, now, and get to work.

This next exercise is very powerful, and all it involves is the imagination. Simply imagine that this is the last moment of your life, and be ready to die. Now. But just before you do that, ask yourself: if this were your last moment, how would you want to be? Would you want to be worried? Would you want to be tense or relaxed? Would you want to be angry or forgiving? Would you like to be frowning or smiling? And what image would you like to have on your mind? What posture would you like to adopt: slouched or standing? Sitting down or dancing?

To make this exercise even more powerful, consider one of these three assumptions, whichever suits your own beliefs: *How you die in this life will determine how you will be born in the next one.* (This assumption is inspired by the Eastern philosophy of karma.) Or try this one: *The state of your soul when you die determines how you will spend eternity.* (This assumption is inspired by the Biblical idea of divine justice.) Or try this one: *Imagine that a snapshot of your soul is taken at the moment you die, and this image will be posted on the Internet. All other records and memories of you will be deleted.* (This more modern assumption is inspired by science fiction, but should certainly do the trick.)

I'm sure you can see that, whichever starting assumption you choose for your ending, it will bring you directly to your most essential self. The idea behind this exercise is that you already have access to your highest, deepest nature, so why wait until you're almost dead to experience it? Why not live from it now?

You can do this exercise many times throughout the day. I do it whenever I am especially reminded of death: when I pass a traffic accident, when the plane I'm on is taking off or landing, when I visit someone in the hospital, when I say goodbye at the train station, or when I hear about a natural disaster. I use each of these experiences to remind myself that I could die right now. This usually causes me to sit up straight, for I don't want to die slouched, and to open my heart, for I don't want to die uptight. The benefit is that, in the next moment, if I'm still alive, I am just a little bit more upright and a little bit more loving.

> Imagine that this is your very last moment.
> How would you like to be? See if you can put
> your body in that position and your soul
> in that condition. Try it right now. Try it
> whenever you are reminded of death.

Beginning

Once, on a transatlantic flight, I had the delightful experience of playing a version of peek-a-boo with a five-year-old boy sitting in the seat in front of me. He would duck down behind the seat, wait a few seconds, then suddenly pop up. Each time he did this, he seemed delighted to see me again, as if for the first time. He loved making me believe that he had, for a moment, disappeared. (That I pretended to believe this each time helped considerably.) We played this game, on and off, all the way across the Atlantic.

Peek-a-boo is a game that helps children learn about continuity, for newborn babies don't take continuity for granted. They need to be reassured constantly that a loving, supportive presence exists around them. They can only play peek-a-boo when they are fairly certain that there is some continuity to themselves and the world; otherwise, it would be too terrifying. So for young children, playing peek-a-boo is a way of practicing and reinforcing their newfound sense of continuity: even when Mother's eyes are covered, she's still here. For older children, such as the boy I described, peek-a-boo is a playful remembering of the time when continuity wasn't taken for granted.

As we get older, we take continuity so much for granted that we forget that discontinuity is possible. The only discontinuity we can imagine is death, and we try very hard not to think about that. It could even be said that we have become addicted to continuity—especially our own—as if we believed that life should go forward, in a straight line, to infinity. We try to live as long as possible, and we even try to extend life—through our offspring and achievements—past death.

But holding ourselves together from one moment to the next, in a straight line, creates a lot of tension, for if we are extending ourselves over time, we're overextended. Continuity itself is a kind of tension. But if we can open ourselves up to discontinuity, we can find some liberation. To experience discontinuity (after you have mastered continuity) means that you really know that, in the next moment, everything could be different. You stop taking life for granted.

So right now, imagine that you are playing peek-a-boo with the world. Just close your eyes, and then open them, quickly. Imagine that you are seeing the world for the first time. What do you notice? What draws your attention? How do you feel?

In doing this, the more you pretend that you are a child, astonished by the return of the world, the more you will get out of it. Try closing your eyes for a little longer, or squeezing your eyes a little tighter. Try popping them open suddenly, opening them as wide as possible, with a surprised expression on your face. Look around at the new world that has suddenly appeared.

Do this now. Play peek-a-boo with the world.

This exercise may seem silly at first, but it really works. You can do it whenever you need to refresh your awareness. With this exercise, you will certainly experience more delight in the world. And you will certainly see more in delight.

Managing the Moment

When I was a student at business school, I learned many useful theories about organization, and many good management skills, but the whole idea of management also seemed inconsistent with my spiritual beliefs. Spirituality, to me, was about trust, openness and humility, whereas management seemed to be about prediction and control.

Indeed, many managers operate from fear: the fear that life isn't okay if they aren't managing it. And it's not just managers who have this fear. We all do. We are all managing, or trying to manage, something. We are all at least trying to manage ourselves. It's a vicious cycle: we feel anxious, so we manage more, and the more we manage, the more we worry about what would happen if we didn't manage.

By managing all the time, however, we inhibit the natural flow of creativity. We inhibit the possibility that something unpredictable might happen; then we have trouble adapting when it, invariably, does. We fail to trust the inherent wisdom of the situation and the inherent wisdom of the group. We impose solutions based on models from past experience as if they were absolute rules of life.

If a miracle—or even just a really good new idea—wanted to happen, it would really have to hit us on the head very hard. Otherwise we just wouldn't notice it, or couldn't adapt to it. And yet, every day, a million wonderful new opportunities present themselves to us. The universe is *always* offering us a new way out of our old problems. The universe is changing, moment by moment, and wants us to change with it. New ideas are just dying to be born.

So the next time you feel an impulse to manage: stop. Just do a One-Breath Cycle and see what happens. Do this every time you feel a need to manage—whether you are managing a whole city, a small business, a classroom of children, your family, your partner, or just yourself. See what it's like to stop managing for a moment. See what it's like to spend a moment unmanaging.

Now you may believe that everyone around you wants, needs and expects you to be in control; they want a strong leader. Indeed, you may believe that everyone will panic if you stop managing. But perhaps this is only because they have become dependent on having someone else do the managing. Maybe if you stop managing, they will manage. Maybe if we all stopped managing, we would all manage. Nowadays, in my work with managers, I try to help them discover the rich source of wisdom available in unmanaged moments.

Remember that, despite the best predictive measures in the world, you do not actually know what will happen in the next moment. And you can't really control it. This does not mean that the science of prediction is meaningless, or that we should not plan for the future. It just means that our planning must come from an awareness of constant change and a radical openness to what might be. If we can learn to manage less, or rather, manage from a deep presence in the present, then we will experience less fear and greater possibility.

If we accept that each moment is radically new, and has the potential to surprise us, this means that the next moment is not completely determined by the past. So although you might like to complain that you are a victim of the past, or that you are constrained by the choices that you (and others) have made before, you do not *have* to let your experiences from the past color your present. You can be bitter or hopeful; you can be worn down or optimistic; you can have a closed mind or an open mind.

One of the secrets to letting go of stress is simply admitting that you don't really know what's going on, that you're not really in control, and that even the things you're certain about are always in motion, always changing. This is also the greatest gift you can give to others too: allowing them the freedom to be different from who they were yesterday.

A true master uses every moment of attention to remember how little she knows. She uses every moment of presence to open out to possibility. This is a practice of *not* knowing, and it is the heart of humility. So try adding this to your practice: When you catch yourself about to act like a know-it-all, do a One-Breath Cycle. When you catch yourself about to act from an unquestioned assumption, do a One-Breath Cycle. Return to a state of innocence and remind yourself how little you know. Hold open the possibility that something will be different. Give the world a little space. It will surprise you.

The Turnaround Moment

In the introduction to this book, I said that the word "moment" comes from a Latin word meaning "a particle sufficient to turn the scales," and I used this idea to remind you that each moment has enormous potential. The question, then, is whether you are awake for this opportunity and whether you can use it to turn around even a difficult situation.

Here is a situation that happens many times, each day, in every workplace. One person is under stress—because of a deadline or a performance review or a crisis—and he passes his stress on to someone else or everyone else—especially those at a lower level in the hierarchy. This has a toxic effect on the environment. It leads to bad work, simmering resentment, high blood pressure, and high turnover costs. And it doesn't just happen at work. I'm sure that we all do this, if only a little bit, to someone, sometime. Many parents even do this to their children.

There is another way, however. Try whispering to yourself *"Pssst.* Don't pass it on." In other words, no matter what happens to you, vow not to pass the stress of it on to someone else. No matter what stress you have absorbed, even if it was caused by another person, it's now your responsibility to transform it. Make your own body a vessel of change.

In other words, no matter what happens to you, vow not to pass the stress of it on to anyone else. Do a Portable Minute or a One-Breath Cycle. You might experience the stress dissipating. Or you might find a way to release it appropriately. Or you might find that the stress converts to pure energy, and that this energy spreads throughout your body, becoming a feeling of vitality and empowerment.

If you practice this repeatedly, you will find that other people's stress doesn't stress you as much. And I believe that if we would each stop passing on our stress, there would be less stress coming our way.

Sadly, most people seem to live according to Newton's third law of motion: "For every action there is an equal and opposite reaction." If someone hurts us, we hurt him back—or we hurt someone else instead. But whenever we try "not to pass it on," we are attempting to live in harmony with Christ's teaching, "If someone strikes you on the right cheek, turn to him the other also." We remember that we are not just Newtonian objects, reacting equally and oppositely: we are people, and we can do better. If we could be always prepared with a One-Breath Cycle, then if someone does strike us, we might be able to buy some time. In that moment, we might be able to choose consciously whether to strike back, turn the other cheek, or find another option. Perhaps one moment really could turn the world around.

> Make a small sign that says "Pssst. Don't pass it on." Keep this where you can see it frequently. Instead of reacting to someone else's stress, try a One-Breath Cycle.

The Right Moment

There is a wonderful word in ancient Greek, *kairos*, which means the "right moment." *Kairos* suggests that some moments are just right for some things, and other moments are just right for other things—as in the biblical "To everything there is a season, and a time for every purpose under heaven."

Yet so much of the time, we do things when the time is wrong. We are actually quite unsophisticated in our ability to sense the right time. How much effort is wasted, and blood pressure elevated, by failing to notice when the time is right?

For example, I'm sure you have tried at some point to give advice to a friend and had the strong feeling that your words were wasted. Then, at another time, you say just the right thing and it is extremely helpful: *it gets in*. The trick of giving good advice is not just knowing *what* to say, but *when* to say it. This same principle applies to decision-making: it's not just *what* you do; it's *when* you do it. A master knows the right moment for everything, and so wastes effort on nothing.

For most of my life, I had this completely backwards. I seemed to enjoy pushing when the door was closed, and I lost interest when the door was open. Most people aren't quite so masochistic; they just fail to notice their own rhythms and the rhythms of the world around them. But you can learn to listen more closely to yourself, and learn to read the signals of the world more accurately. You can learn to sense when the time is right. You can learn when to try harder and when to rest. You can learn when to seize the opportunity and when to let it pass.

In the art of archery, *kairos* refers to "an opening, or 'opportunity,' or, more precisely, a long tunnel-like aperture through which the archer's arrow has to pass. Successful passage of a *kairos* requires, therefore, that the archer's arrow be fired not only accurately but with enough power for it to penetrate."[15] This suggests that we need a certain confidence to act in the right moment.

In the art of weaving, *kairos* refers to "the 'critical time' when the weaver must draw the yarn through a gap that momentarily opens in the warp of the cloth being woven."[16] This suggests that you must always be ready for opportunity to knock. Sadly, many of us have such a narrow understanding of our potential that we wouldn't notice opportunity even if it rang the doorbell.

In the New Testament, the word *kairos* is used to mean "the time when God acts." On the highest level, this refers to divine intervention, but on a day-to-day level, this means waiting for the right moment to manifest and make itself clear to you.

I believe that, in any moment, something wants to happen, but this may not be what you consciously want to happen. Mastery means not just knowing how to get what you want, but *listening and watching for what is wanted of you*. This does not need to be a mystical revelation. It simply means listening for the deepest, truest voice within you, as well as paying attention to the spirit of the time.

There is another sense of *kairos*, however, that is deeper still, and this meaning promotes even deeper stillness. If you are waiting for the right moment to experience inner peace, don't. Inner peace can appear when you least expect it, even in the midst of personal stress, a public emergency, or a great tragedy. (I knew a firefighter who experienced his moments of deepest peace in the midst of a burning building.) The point is that when inner peace is the issue, any moment and every moment is the right moment. Every moment is the moment you have been waiting for.

You may be tempted to say, "Sure, I'd love to be peaceful now but you have no idea how busy I am." I have a lot of sympathy for that excuse—I use it quite often. But it makes no sense. First of all, when you are the busiest is when you most need inner peace. And second, it is the very act of postponement—of turning away from the moment that is here—that is the real cause of inner turmoil.

By stopping your mind from creating the fantasy of stillness *in the future*, and accepting the feeling of the stress that you're having, the stress becomes a little easier to handle. And then you are much more likely to be open to the possibility of not being stressed in the next moment.

So just try to be with what is happening now, even if it doesn't feel conducive to being peaceful. Harmonize your breathing with what's happening. You will soon learn that moments of stress are neither interruptions in stillness, nor delays in stillness, but part of its play. You could even say that stress is the way that stillness challenges you to find deeper stillness.

Notice the next time you say to yourself, "I'm too busy right now for a One-Breath Cycle." Then do a One-Breath Cycle immediately.

The Ultimate Moment

I am convinced that all of our problems are somehow related to beliefs about time or space. We feel that time is moving too slowly, that too many things are happening at once, or that we're running out of time. We crave more space, or the ideal space, or we have a conflict with others about space (as in traffic jams or border disputes). It's as if we believed that we should be able to zoom anywhere we want, with no temporal or spatial limitations whatsoever. Nothing should get in our way.

Whenever we do have a conflict involving time or space, our first impulse is usually to curse time ("I don't have enough"), or curse space ("I need some more"), or curse other people who are not acting in accord with our need for time and space—such as that person moving so slowly on the sidewalk in front of you ("If only he would get out of my way"). Or we try to change the conditions in order to get more time or space—we rush or slow down, postpone a deadline, build a new room, put up a fence.

But I want to suggest something radical to you: that everything—absolutely everything—happens at the right time.

This can't be proven, of course. But you can try it out, as a philosophy, and see what happens. You can see what happens if, instead of railing against the time and space, or trying to solve your problem about time and space, you simply trust, for a moment, that the time and space are perfect. You don't have to like what's happening. Indeed sometimes it will feel awful—perfectly awful. But just see what happens if you accept, for a moment, that the time and place are exactly right.

Whenever you come into conflict with time or space, this is a moment of great opportunity. Instead of rushing or stalling or cursing, simply consider that the timing is perfect and the space is sufficient, do a One-Breath Cycle, and see what changes.

I believe that every experience of conflict—between you and time, between you and space, between you and other people, or between you and the whole world—is an invitation for you to take a moment. In fact, the most opportune time to take a moment is precisely when you feel the timing's all wrong.

> The next time you feel a conflict about time,
> that the timing "isn't right" or "is all
> wrong," consider that the timing is actually
> perfect—you just don't know yet why or how.
> Then do a One-Breath Cycle immediately.

With this exercise, you might first experience just a little more peacefulness: instead of struggling against the conflict, you breathe right in the heart of the conflict. You become a little less conflicted about the conflict. Then you might experience an inkling that there is something to be learned here, or that this misfortune might be happening for some reason. In the Abrahamic traditions, this idea is known as God's will. God's will is not always clear to us, nor does it always make sense, but it always gives us an opportunity to trust God more deeply. In the Eastern traditions, this derives from the idea of karma: every moment is a perfect opportunity for you to learn an important lesson.

The next thing you might experience is the one thing that ever really heals a conflict with time or space, and that is love. When you love someone, it is impossible to say "you" or "me." In love, you are less your "self" and the other person is less the "other." Love is what appears when you stop perceiving a boundary between yourself and the other. It is also the experience that, in reality, there are no boundaries. And the deepest form of love, which could be called Love, is not just for someone close to you, but for everyone and everything. This Love occurs when you realize that you and the world are not really separate—that there is just one thing taking different forms, ceaselessly.

Whenever you move beyond the conflict between you and space, or between you and time, you experience this Love. For Love is not an occasional overwhelming experience, but the nature of reality. It is simply what you experience when the apparent boundary between you and the world—the apparent grid of space and time—dissolves.

Whenever you feel Love, you are truly in the moment. Said philosopher Alfred North Whitehead, "[Love] does not look to the future; for it finds its own reward in the immediate present."[17] In other words, whenever you are experiencing Love, there is no time and there is no space.

I'll go one step further: you can't truly be in the moment without feeling at least an inkling of Love. This may not be a big, overwhelming emotion: it could be quite subtle. It might just be the love of what you're doing. Or the simple love of being. If you're very lucky, it is the love of being doing, and doing being.

In the experience of Love, time and space simply stop being a problem. You stop counting, you stop comparing, and you stop measuring. In the words of Proust, "Love is space and time as measured directly by the heart." In the experience of Love, space and time dissolve, and so do you.

A Moment of Appreciation

Before closing Part 7, I would like to enjoy a Moment of Appreciation. A Moment of Appreciation can be enjoyed whenever you become aware of what is happening and you want to make sure that you appreciate it.

Whenever a moment seems special to us—for example, when we're travelling and we see a famous monument or stunning landscape, when we're at a wedding or birthday or other celebration, or when we see our children looking especially cute—we tend to reach for a camera to "capture" that moment. Unfortunately, we reach for the camera so quickly that we end up taking photos of experiences that we've hardly even experienced. This reflexive reaching for the camera can interrupt our *experience* of the moment. Capturing the moment can sometimes kill it.

If you'd like to try an alternative, consider a Moment of Appreciation. A Moment of Appreciation is a One-Breath Cycle done in a spirit of appreciation, very slowly, and with this slight modification: as you inhale, imagine that you are breathing *in* the experience—with its associated feelings—and imprinting this on your mind; as you exhale, imagine that you're breathing *out* the experience.

Notice that, in this exercise, you are definitely not "capturing" the moment: you are appreciating it fully *and* releasing it fully. You are appreciating *this* moment, but also making room for the *next* one. A Moment of Appreciation doesn't stop the flow of life at all.

A Moment of Appreciation can also be helpful when life seems to be going too fast . . . and slowing down just isn't an option. My friend Clara Britton took a Moment of Appreciation—several of them, in fact—during the birth of her child. After a difficult pregnancy and a long labor, suddenly the delivery began to go *very* quickly. But Clara didn't feel ready for it. She wanted a break—just to catch up emotionally with what was happening. She wanted a pause to honor the transition, say goodbye to her pregnancy and be fully ready to meet her child. But, of course, she couldn't stop the labor. Her only option was to breathe with what was happening and to be fully present, emotionally and spiritually, in the flow of it—moment by moment.

Her story is a good reminder that we can be fully present in a moment even as it's speeding by. We don't need to stop the action; we just need to see it differently. In the movies, this change of perception—a kind of heightened awareness—is often shown in slow motion. Although something dramatic is happening quickly, the protagonist seems to be experiencing it very slowly, taking in all the details, registering them fully. Living in the moment is a lot like this—as if you could flip a mental switch to slow motion at will, and notice the nuance of life—as it's flying by.

But perhaps the most remarkable Moments of Appreciation arise spontaneously, for no reason at all, when you are doing something very ordinary. You suddenly appreciate the world as it is, in its ordinariness. You appreciate the miracle that anything exists at all, and you even appreciate the miracle of your own existence. You appreciate that you exist, appreciating. I do hope that this book has helped you—and continues to help you—experience many such moments.

Please take a Moment of Appreciation now.

PART 8
Mastering the Moment

The No-Moment Moment

In order to master the moment, you must take one small, final step. But before you can do that, I must explain a certain paradox of the moment, a paradox that you may have noticed popping up at various points in this book. I'm going to try to explain it now, but please understand that a paradox, by definition, can't really be explained.

From one perspective, each moment flows seamlessly into the next. In this view, time is *continuous*. Spiritual teachers who take this view remind us that, although we like to think things are permanent or last a long time, in reality, nothing does. We just *believe* things are fixed, solid, or have duration over time, but they are really always changing, and nothing ever stays itself. Whereas stress is the result of trying to hold on to a sense of permanence, peacefulness manifests when you let go of the illusion that anything in life is permanent—including you. So don't cling to anything: not your job, your partner, your house or even your ideas about yourself—just "go with the flow." In other words, reality is all "go."

From another perspective, however, there is no such thing as change. In any moment, you only see the world as it is, now. For example, you never see one leaf falling from a tree:

first you see a leaf on a tree, then in the next moment you see a leaf in the air, and then in the next moment you see a leaf on the ground. All you ever really experience is a static "now" point. So in other words, now is all there is. In this experience of time, there is no bridge between moments, for time is *discontinuous*. Spiritual teachers who take this view suggest that time—and the perception that things change—is the illusion. When we drop this illusion, we experience the present moment fully, for the present moment is all there is. And in letting go of any ideas of past and future, and even the existence of past and future, we touch eternity. So in other words, reality is profoundly still.

So from one perspective, everything changes, and from the other perspective, there is no change. From one perspective, time flows, and from the other perspective, there is no time. From one perspective, there is no now, and from the other perspective, there is only now. From one perspective, reality is continuous, and from the other perspective, reality is discontinuous. From one perspective, everything is in motion, and from the other perspective, everything is still.

The great Zen teacher, Eihei Dogen, summed up this paradoxical nature of reality with his challenging phrase "continuous discontinuity." Perhaps a more user-friendly description would be this:

The only thing that doesn't change
is that everything changes.

This is an unsettling notion, if you consider it. Whenever I reflect on it, I feel a bit wobbly—as if there were no ground to stand on. And yet this wobbly feeling is also a wonderful feeling. It is dynamic and full of energy. It is surprisingly liberating and, also, very peaceful. We could also express it this way:

**In order to experience complete stillness,
you must completely accept that
everything is on the go.**

Notice that, whichever way you look at it, there is no such thing as *one* moment. From one perspective, which regards everything as constantly changing, moments are *constantly* changing, so there is no *one* moment apart from another. From the other perspective, which perceives that nothing is changing, then there isn't *one* moment distinguishable from any other moment because there *aren't* any other moments: there is only now, eternally.

In his book *No Boundary* philosopher Ken Wilber puts it this way: "Because there is no past and no future outside this now-moment, there are no boundaries to this moment—nothing came before it, nothing comes after it. You never experience a beginning to it; you never experience an end to it."[18] He then quotes the Buddhist *Platform Sutra*:

In this moment there is nothing which comes to be. In this moment there is nothing which ceases to be . . . .

[T]here is no boundary or limit to this moment, and herein is eternal delight.[19]

This brings me to some bad news, however. Since the moment has no before or after, there is no such thing as *one* moment apart from any other moment. And if there is no such thing as one moment, then you certainly can't master it. You will never be able to sit back at some time in the future, reminisce about the One-Moment Method, and think "done that." In other words, mastery requires constant renewal. Mastery means always starting again, as if for the first time.

So if you ever think that you have already become a master, you have stepped out of the moment. If you think that you will become a master at some time in the future, you have also stepped out of the moment. And if you ever meet someone who claims to be a master *all the time,* he has truly missed the point: you can only be a master momentarily. Which brings me to the good news:

Although you can't be a master forever,
you can certainly be a master right now.

The Momentary Master

The ancient Chinese book of wisdom *The Book of Change* says that, for the wise person, "time is only significant in that, within it, the steps of becoming can unfold in clearest sequence." In other words, time is not a prison but an opportunity. It is the loom on which you weave your life, the classroom in which you learn your lessons, the playground in which you discover and express your possibility. The point is not to be free from time but to be in time, freely. Mastery is when you accept, moment by moment, everything that happens to you in time, for you know that it's just part of the territory.

If you can accept that time is not as real as you thought, but a wonderful opportunity, then you are actually free to enjoy time passing. Time is no longer the enemy or something in short supply. You are no longer in a tragic-comic battle to get the better of time, and you no longer believe you're a victim of time. You don't need to be "still," and you are no longer "on the go." There is no hurry, and there is no fear. It's okay to be young, and it's okay to be old, for you are just "being time."

With the life experience of an elder and the innocence of a child, you accept everything arising right now as what it is. For now you know that *now* is where it's at, and that *now* is beyond measure. In his poem "This We Have Now" Rumi put it this way:

This we have now
is not imagination.

This is not
grief or joy.

Not a judging state,
or an elation,
or sadness.

Those come
and go.

This is the presence
that doesn't.[20]

In this now, you see everything as if for the first time. In the Christian tradition, this now was described by Meister Eckhart as the "now of eternity, where the soul in God knows all things fresh and new." In the Buddhist tradition, it was invoked by Zen teacher Taizan Maezumi whenever he ordained a new monk. Sprinkling a few drops of water over the newly shaved head of a novitiate, he would proclaim, "Everything is fresh and new!"

And this "now" is now yours, too. In each and every moment, when you discover the world—and yourself—all over again, you are a master. For in this moment, both momentary and momentous, you know that:

> With this breath, I am reborn
> And everything is fresh and new.

Notes

1. Rumi, Jalal al-din, *The Essential Rumi*, Coleman Barks (trans.), (San Francisco: HarperSanFrancisco, 1995), p.260.

2. *The Chambers Dictionary* (Edinburgh: Chambers Harrap Publishers Ltd., 1998), p.416.

3. Browne, Ivor, "Psychological Trauma, or Unexperienced Experience," *ReVision*, 12 (1990).

4. Davies, Paul, "That Mysterious Flow," *Scientific American Special*, Volume 16, Number 1, 2006, p.7.

5. See Fernandez-Armesto, Felipe, "Time and History," in Lippincott, Kristin, ed., *The Story of Time* (London: Merrell Holberton Publishers, Ltd., 1999), p.248.

6. Ibid., pp. 248–9.

7. Quoted in Davies, op. cit.

8. Davies, Paul, *About Time* (London: Penguin, 1995), p.10. Used by permission of Simon & Schuster, Inc., New York.

9. Barbour, Julian, *The End of Time* (London: Phoenix, div. of Orion Publishing Group, 2000) p.137. Used by permission of Oxford University Press, Inc.

10. W., Bill, *Three Talks to Medical Societies by Bill W., co-founder of A.A.* (New York: Alcoholics Anonymous World Services; 2006), p.14. The excerpt from the pamphlet "Three talks to Medical Societies by Bill W. co-founder of A.A." is a reprinted with permission of Alcoholics Anonymous World Services, Inc (AAWS). Permission to reprint the excerpt does not mean that AAWS has reviewed or approved the contents of this publication, or that AAWS necessarily agrees with the views expressed herein. A.A is a program of recov-

ery from alcoholism only—use of the excerpt in connection with programs and activities which are patterned after A.A., but which address other problems, or in any other non A.A. context, does not imply otherwise.

11. Parks, Rosa, as told to Greenshaw, Wayne, *The Thunder of Angels*, with Donnie Williams (Chicago: Lawrence Hill Books, 2005).

12. Mitchell, Stephen, trans., *Bhagavad Gita* (London: Rider & Co., 2000), pp. 135, 140.

13. Tillich, Paul, *The Shaking of the Foundations* (New York: Charles Scribner's Sons, 1950), pp.161–2.

14. Cooper, David, *God Is a Verb: Kabbalah and the Practice of Mystical Judaism* (New York: Riverhead Books, 1997), p.62.

15. White, Eric Charles, *Kaironomia: On the Will-to-Invent* (Ithaca: Cornell University Press, 1987, quoted in "Composing the Present Moment," Judge, Anthony, http://www.laetusinpraesens.org/doc/ficino.php

16. Ibid.

17. Whitehead, Alfred North, in Sherburne, Donald W., ed., *A Key to Whitehead's Process and Reality* (Chicago: University of Chicago Press, 1981), p.179.

18. Wilber, Ken, *No Boundary* (Boston and London: Shambhala, 1985), p.69.

19. Cited in Ibid., p.69.

20. Rumi, Jalal al-din, *The Essential Rumi*, Coleman Barks (trans.), (San Francisco: HarperSanFrancisco, 1995), p.261.

The author would like to thank the following for permission to use copyright material: Alcoholics Anonymous World Services for material from "Three Talks to Medical Societies by Bill W." (see Note 10 for more information); Coleman Barks for lines from *The Essential Rumi* (San Francisco: HarperSanFrancisco, 1995), trans. Coleman Barks; Wayne Greenshaw for lines quoted in *The Thunder of Angels*, with Donnie Williams (Chicago: Lawrence Hill Books, 2005); Simon & Schuster, Inc. for material from *About Time* by Paul Davies (New York: Simon &

Schuster, Inc., 1995); Oxford University Press, Inc. for material from *The End of Time* by Julian Barbour; Rider, an imprint of Ebury Publishing and Random House, and Harmony Books, a division of Random House, Inc., for lines from *Bhagavad Gita*, trans. Stephen Mitchell (London: Rider, 2000); Riverhead Books, a division of the Penguin Group Inc, for material from David Cooper, *God is A Verb* (New York: Riverhead Books, 1997), p.62; Scientific American for material from "That Mysterious Flow" by Paul Davies in *Scientific American Special*, vol. 16, 2006; Shambhala Publications for material form *No Boundary* by Ken Wilber (Boston and London: Shambhala, 1985): Dr Mutie Tillich-Farris for the material from *The Shaking of the Foundations* by Paul Tillich (New York: Charles Scribner's Sons,1950); Eric Charles White for material from *Kaironomia: On the Will-to-Invent* (Ithaca: Cornell University Press, 1987). Every effort has been made to trace and credit all copyright holders but if any have been inadvertently overlooked the author and publisher will be pleased to make the necessary arrangement at the first opportunity.

Acknowledgements

Many friends, family members, and teachers read the first draft of this book and gave me invaluable suggestions. Deep thanks to: Florence Boroson, Louis Boroson, Andrew Dodd, Randall Ryotan Eiger Sensei, Lenny Gibson, Nienke Merbis, Barbara Joshin O'Hara Sensei, Ryah Parker, Doug Paxton, Kris Stone, Diana Theodores, and Elise Thoron. My sister, Barbara Boroson, provided particularly generous and careful criticism, indispensible copyediting, and much encouragement, as always. My brother-in-law, Joseph Rutt, provided calm essential advice in the publication process.

Sugra Zaman helped me turn my initial ideas into a book proposal, and then find a first home for the book at Rider. At Rider, I am grateful to Judith Kendra, Publishing Director, for her sensitive editing of the initial manuscript, Sue Lascelles for help in copyediting, and Catherine Trippett, for solving an important permissions problem.

Thank you also to Jacky Sach, a wise and careful agent, Whitney Lee for helping this book find publication in many languages, and Jill Mangino for her enthusiastic advice and publicity. I am grateful to Nigel Westwood for his design help, have truly enjoyed working and playing with Sue Snell on the cover design, and feel especially fortunate to have had this edition designed by Level C.

In addition to those cited in the Notes, several articles and books provided essential background reading for me. *The Story of Time*, edited by Kristen Lippincott, is a fascinating and diverse collection of essays that was essential for Part 3. My attempt to penetrate the paradoxes of time was greatly aided by Eihei Dogen's *Shobogenzo*, Stephen Heine's *Existential and Ontological Dimensions of Time in Heidegger and Dogen*, and Donald Sherburne's *Companion to Whitehead's Process and Reality*. Stan Grof's The *Cosmic Game* and Duane Elgin's writings on continuous creation were helpful for Part 7.

Thank you too to Nienke Merbis, Ed Merbis, Jean Farrell and Bill Farrell for holding such a loving space for the years of exploration from which this book emerged. Thank you too to Michael Harris and Jo Hardy for their help during some critical blocks in the flow. My parents' enthusiasm for everything I undertake has been a huge resource for me, and I am so grateful to them. And I am so grateful to my partner, Andrew Dodd, for his inspirational drive for excellence, his constant support, his astute advice, and the joy he brings to my life. Thank you, too, to Toby and his Ma, who look after us so well.

Finally, I thank Roshi Enkyo O'Hara and all the members of the Village Zendo in New York. With their compassionate and playful presence, right here in the world, they have helped me—and this book—more than they know.

About the Author

MARTIN BOROSON studied Western philosophy at Yale and earned an MBA from the Yale School of Management. He then set out to learn other ways of knowing—through psychology, spiritual practice and the arts. He studied Eastern philosophy, trained in transpersonal psychology with Dr. Stanislav Grof, and founded the arts production company, The Temenos Project. Martin now brings these approaches together as an organizational consultant, helping companies and communities that want a broad-based approach to innovation and decision-making. He provides training in one-moment meditation in public workshops, leadership seminars, and the media. He can be reached at www.martinboroson.info.

For additional exercises, resources,
and momentary reminders by email:

www.onemomentmeditation.net

3033559

Made in the USA